You
Don't Have
to Be Thin
to Win

The Official
Chub Club Coach's
Workout Program

You
Don't Have
to Be Thin
to Win

Judy Molnar
with Bob Babbitt

Villard / New York

No book, including this one, can ever replace the advice of a qualified physician. Please consult your doctor before beginning this or any other exercise program.

Library of Congress Cataloging-in-Publication Data
Molnar, Judy.
    You don't have to be thin to win: the official Chub Club Coach's workout
    program / Judy Molnar with Bob Babbitt.
        p. cm.
    ISBN 0-375-50414-1
    1. Molnar, Judy. 2. Rosie O'Donnell Show. 3. Women—Health and
    hygiene. 4. Physical fitness for women. 5. Exercise for women.
    I. Babbitt, Bob. II. Title.
    RA778.M687 2000
    613.7′045—dc21   99-048598

Random House website address: www.atrandom.com

Printed in the United States of America on acid-free paper

9 8 7 6 5 4 3 2

First Edition

BOOK DESIGN BY BARBARA MARKS

I dedicate this book to my mom and dad, Evelyn and Emery Molnar, who have given me my life and constant love and support in all my pursuits. You have always guided me to do my personal best. Thanks for always being there for me (even sitting through my fifth-grade orchestra concerts).

Foreword

by Rosie O'Donnell

If you had told me in January 1999 that I would finish a 5K mini-marathon in Central Park the following May, I would have picked up my Devil Dog and told you to get psychiatric help. Then I met Judy Molnar.

While most fitness people intimidate me, I immediately felt comfortable with Judy. Okay, maybe the fact that she had competed in the Ironman Triathalon was a little intimidating, but on the other hand it was inspiring. Here was this formerly big person who had figured out how to take care of herself. She has a simple philosophy—eat less, move more. All of a sudden diet and exercise took on human dimensions—these were terms I could understand.

Through the Chub Club, Judy was able to help thousands of people. She gave us goals that were attainable. As opposed to diving into deprivation and boot camp, we could start being healthier in small steps—one less doughnut, one more flight of stairs. Little by little it all adds up.

On May 23, 1999, at the Toys "R" Us 5K, Judy showed up and could see how many lives she had affected. Over 12,000 Chub Club members—leaner and meaner than in January—finished the race. They ate a little less, they moved a little more, and they felt good about their accomplishments.

So put down that doughnut and pick up this book. See how easy that is? It's the first step, and that one's always the hardest.

Acknowledgments

First, my thanks to my mom and dad, who have been the best in being there for me at all my games, theater performances, and so much more. Thanks for being such wonderful and supportive parents.

Thanks also to my sister and brothers, their spouses, and my nieces and nephews: Jeanne, Frank, Emery, Mary Beth, Elise, Emery, Jack, Michael, Roberta, Mallory, Mariah, Meredith, Muerille, Mikey, Thomas, Beth, and Joey. Thanks for always taking time to call, write, and be there at special events. Your encouragement over the past few years has made my life easier. Our time together is precious.

To Rick, my loving, supportive boyfriend and future. You have been the source of my strength with words of wisdom and constant cheerleading. It is with you I have found the meaning of love and patience. Life is not complete without you there. Two peas in a pod.

To my aunt Marge Heineman, who has shown me the true spirit of competing as a woman athlete. And thanks for your inspiration at sixty-three years old and still participating in the Senior Games.

To Ross Products Division, the makers of Ensure, especially Marianne Spain, Kerry Hurff, Rhonda Peterson, and Barb Renico, for being a wonderful client and great support team.

To Keith Fernbach from Alan-Taylor Communications for getting my story out there.

To World Triathlon Corporation, organizer of the Ironman Triathlon World Championship, Lew Friedland, Sharron Ackles, Ken Murrah, Priscilla Fraiegari, and all the great staff. Thanks for finding value not only in my story but in me as well.

To Terence Noonan, human interest producer at *The Rosie O'Donnell Show,* for booking me on the show twice. "This Is the Moment," sung by Broadway star Robert Cuccioli, was a wonderful surprise and gift.

To Rosie and *The Rosie O'Donnell Show* for allowing me to share a message of hope that you can have a healthy lifestyle.

To Scott Waxman for making the deal happen with this book and for your constant words of encouragement as we made the rounds.

Acknowledgments

To Bob Babbitt and Beth Hagman for taking time from your summer to make the words of the book appear on the page. And, Bob, remember you still got to play your Xtreme Golf each morning!

To Mollie Doyle, who has been such a great joy to work with. Thanks for sharing your personal fitness experience and professional experience in making this book come to life, and the folks at Villard, especially Beth Pearson and Joanne Barracca.

To Troy Jacobson for taking me from the couch to participating in triathlons. Your coaching and guidance in the beginning has helped me to go further.

To the folks at the Multisport School of Champions in Boulder, Colorado, for making me realize what it means to do an Ironman. I appreciate having the opportunity in June 1999 to participate in a week of training and learning with John Duke, Paula Newby-Fraser, Paul Huddle, Roch Frey, Slice, Peter Reid, and Lori Bowden. You made sure I never got dropped and have given me new confidence.

To Paula Newby-Fraser, Helen Keilholtz, and Shannon Delaney for allowing me to be part of the Iron Girl experience in designing athletic clothing for full-figured women that is feminine and functional. Your support is priceless!

To my friend Julie Kling, who, as a mother of three, demonstrates to me over and over the spirit of Ironman and competing (even training in New York City). Thanks for the shopping trips, too.

To Teri Gersonde, who has been a wonderful friend and coworker. Thanks for always being there for me over the years.

To Heidi and Bill Sodetz, who have been great friends and training partners. Thanks for always waiting for me on the long rides.

To Glenn Armstrong for being a wonderful support and for teaching me the basics of cycling. (Okay, so not as much big gearing!)

To Bill Bell, at seventy-six years old a true Ironman who is a great inspiration to me. I hope to walk the parade with you again.

To Johnson-Rauhoff, my former employer for eight terrific years.

To Judy Sackfield, my former assistant volleyball coach at Clemson University. Thanks for believing in me and helping me achieve a new level of being an athlete.

To Judy Gentry and John Peakes for taking a chance on me. Thanks for helping me develop my talents as an actress while I did my Actors Equity professional internship at the Boarshead Theater.

Finally, to Amanda, Jim, and Brian, my best friends from high school, who always saw me for who I was.

Contents

Contents

You
Don't Have
to Be Thin
to Win

CHAPTER 1

How Did I Get Here? The Story of How I Went from Fat to Fit

What lies behind us and what lies before us are small matters compared to what lies within us.

—RALPH WALDO EMERSON

How does someone go from a volleyball scholarship to Clemson to morbidly obese in the span of about seven years? Well, it didn't take just seven years. It took a lifetime.

As a youngster growing up in Indiana, I never thought of myself as big and tall. I remember writing a paper on Babe Didrikson in grammar school. She was amazing—a track-and-field star and a great golfer. It seems she could do anything she wanted whenever she wanted. And she was big. I was already big for my age, so I could relate. People started calling me "Babe." I liked that. I thought big was a good thing, something to aspire to.

I was a big girl, but I wasn't the tubby kid who

was abused throughout school. I just had a large frame. I didn't hide out. People always thought I was older because I was tall. I did it all: snowball wars and sports with the guys; playing Barbies in the afternoon. The summer after sixth grade, I worked at Camp Millhouse, a summer camp for physically and mentally challenged kids. The girl who introduced me to the camp couldn't stand being there and left after three days. I ended up working there for three summers.

At first, I was a counselor-in-training, but by the second summer I was leading groups and had all the responsibilities of a full-fledged counselor. I loved every single minute of it. These kids needed me. To make an autistic child laugh or put a smile on a sad child's face made the experience special. The age range was from kindergarten to adult. Even early on, I had as much responsibility as the high school kids. I think it was because I was so tall that I looked mature. Again, I perceived big as a positive state.

In eighth grade, I was the only girl on the boys' baseball team, although I got into only two games and spent more time keeping score than actually wearing a glove or swinging a bat. But I was on the team, and it was an honor.

We moved to Granger, a community outside South Bend, Indiana, that year. Life was good.

I had nicknames in middle school—"Magilla Gorilla," "Grape Ape," "Too Tall Jones"—but I never found them offensive. In ninth grade, one of my teammates started calling me "BJ," or "Big Judy." It had a nice ring to it. To me there wasn't anything negative about it. These were my friends.

I wanted to be a better basketball player. Since I was living near South Bend, the home of Notre Dame, I started watching the Notre Dame basketball team practice. I became an instant fan. Every day I watched and learned from coach Digger Phelps. The practices were closed to the public, but Digger let me sit in.

Me (far left) at the Junior Olympics in 1979—I was already taller than my coach!

I played varsity sports, studied drama, and sang in the choir. I had a ton of friends, and not once do I remember anyone calling me fat. Dating? We all went out as a group, and the boys and girls group-danced together. We even invented our own weekend court dances on the campus of Notre Dame. We took a boom box and went out and danced. I didn't have a special boyfriend, but I always had a secret crush on one of my best friends, Jim. I never felt left out. I even went to my senior prom with Jim, and we had the time of our lives.

I have one sister and three brothers. Jeanne is eight years older than I am, Emery is five years older, Michael is four years older, and Thomas is two years younger. I was one of the tallest in the family. My mom is only five-foot-four, but my father and all my siblings are five-foot-ten and up. At six-foot-one, I was as tall or taller than them all, except Michael, who is six-foot-three.

Me with my brothers and mom in 1983.

My dad has said that I inherited his large frame. I never saw that as a disadvantage, because of my success in sports. Although Jeanne wasn't into sports, my brothers and I were. We got a lot of encouragement from my dad, who had played football and basketball in high school and college. He'd grown up in South Bend and played guard for the first high school basketball champions from that town—South Bend Central.

On the weekends, my brothers and I would watch sports with my dad. I think sports really brought us together. My dad worked with me on positioning for rebounds. I loved to practice shooting, but I hated to run sprints. (People who knew me then are amazed that this girl who just despised running is now running marathons and racing triathlons.)

I always played sports, and I was always the tallest kid in the class. Whenever we lined up for class pictures, there I was—back row, dead center.

Because I was so tall, all the coaches were interested in me. I competed in the high jump, played volleyball and basketball, and took ballet classes. Don't laugh. I wasn't exactly a swan, but ballet was good for me. I remember my ballet teacher

My height gave me an advantage in sports, particularly volleyball and basketball.

With my dad and my sister Jeanne for my high school graduation—I was big, but not fat.

telling me that I had really good posture for a tall girl. I guess most tall women slump, but my mom would tell me to stand up straight because people would look up to me. Height does give you a certain aura, as it makes you look older and conveys a sense of strength.

I remember the track coach trying to get me to throw the shot put and discus. But the idea of bulking up and emphasizing my size even more was not appealing, so I turned him down.

I always wanted to be well rounded and balanced. Some of my coaches had a problem with that because they wanted me to focus on one sport. They said that if I would just concentrate on basketball, I could get a scholarship to college. I wanted that scholarship. But I also wanted more out of life than just sports.

It's ironic that I ended up getting a volleyball scholarship, because my high school volleyball coach wanted to cut me after my junior year. She gave me a three-by-five-inch index card that said I had to improve my work ethic and certain skill areas, or I was history. I worked hard to meet her standards, and it paid off.

College Changed Everything

I went to Clemson on a volleyball scholarship. I was six-foot-one, and I worked hard. I wasn't a natural talent, but I had the heart and enthusiasm to overcome my lack of speed and inability to jump. Judy Sackfield, the assistant coach who recruited me, believed in my potential. We practiced twice a day, every day. She ran with me every morning and did weights with me every afternoon. I lived and breathed volleyball. I was squatting a tremendous amount of weight and kept my own weight between 185 and 200 pounds most of the time.

Unfortunately, Judy left to coach at Georgia Tech during my freshman year, and the head coach had an entirely different philosophy. I was no longer a woman with potential. I was now a large woman with a weight problem.

Suddenly, I was fat. I was expected to weigh in every week at 155 pounds. At the time, I was 180 and very fit. There was no way in the world that I could shrink my body down to the size he wanted. Heck, the last time I had weighed that was probably in middle school. The strength coach, Gary Wade, was my sounding board and tried to help me as much as he could. But I wanted a quick fix, and he had only long-term solutions. I went to the student health center for help. The doctor handed me a twelve-hundred-calorie diet and said, "Eat this." There was no way I could follow that diet.

For the first time in my life, I was a prisoner of the dreaded scale. I tried the Pop-Tarts diet. All I ate for days was Pop-Tarts. Then I tried the grapefruit diet. I hung out with the wrestlers and learned about diuretics and other tricks of the trade: Wear a rubber suit and sweat water weight off.

During my junior year of college, feeling good.

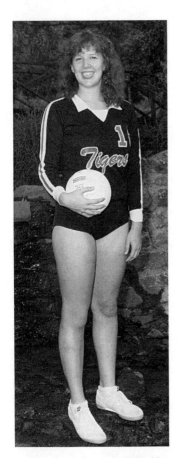

Here I am at 175 pounds. I felt healthy, but the coach wanted me to get down to 150.

Stand to the back of the scale to make yourself appear lighter. Put your hand up on the wall and divert some of the weight from the scale. I became an expert at deceiving the scale.

Back then, body fat testing would have been great for me, as the scale didn't tell the whole story. I put myself on an extreme workout program of running and lifting weights. Then at midseason during my sophomore year, I sprained my ankle badly and spent a lot of time in the trainer's room, trying to get healthy and skinny.

Back then, the "no pain, no gain" theory of sports was practiced. Stopping for water was a sign of weakness, and running in one-hundred-degree heat was a sign of strength. The sports medical community has certainly changed dramatically over the past ten years.

My parents didn't know any of this. I kept it all to myself. People would tell me how good I looked, but the scale told me a totally different story. Unfortunately, the only story my coach wanted to hear was the numbers on the scale.

I started to hate training and working out. Being fit didn't feel good anymore. I was hungry and frustrated all the time. I quit the team after my sophomore year, forfeited my scholarship because I knew I couldn't make their weight requirement, and took a semester off.

When I went back to school, the last thing I wanted to do was anything physical. I got involved in student government, in acting, and in my classes. I put fitness on the back burner. When I left school, I was hired by an advertising agency and learned what it was like to be chained to a desk. My downward fitness spiral accelerated.

I Became a Couch Potato

It happened so gradually. I was bored and stressed, and food became an outlet. Lunchtime was the highlight of my day. On top of that, the company I worked for was the ad agency for a doughnut company that paid us partly in cash and partly in product. By 10:30 A.M. each day, I'd already eaten five or six doughnuts.

I ate when I was happy. I ate when I was sad. Eating became my main activity. Rather than deal with emotions, rather than quit a job that didn't suit me, rather than get out of a bad situation, I stayed where I was and used food as the great comforter.

From 1989 to 1996, my life was dominated by food. Sometimes I would stop at a fast-food restaurant for a breakfast sandwich on my way to work. Then I would consume doughnuts throughout the morning. If I ate lunch at a fast-food restaurant, everything was value size. If I went out with coworkers to a sit-down meal, I always ordered high-fat foods. I never made healthy choices. Often I snacked on candy throughout the day. My boss always had chocolate in her desk drawer. Sometimes she would even send me on a Fannie May candy store run. I usually ate dinner in the car on my way to a meeting or a theater rehearsal. Sometimes the office would order in dinner, usually pizza.

I was involved in theater, the community, and so many activities that I learned to focus on who I was and not necessarily on how much I weighed. My participation in the Twin City Players in St. Joseph was a source of creativity, joy,

This is me at the height of my weight, when I was eating five or six doughnuts for breakfast.

This was at the office Halloween party. Notice where I am: the food table.

and frustration. Because of my height and continued weight gain, the roles that I could play were limited. When I started training with professional acting teachers in Chicago, I was told that my weight and size would get in the way.

I auditioned for a professional theater in Lansing, Michigan, called the Boarshead Theater, and won one of its internship slots. While working there, I learned so much about the craft of acting, but I was always painfully aware that with my height and weight, I didn't fit any of the typical roles for the stage. I stuck out like a sore thumb among the lean leading ladies, and I yearned to be like them. Most embarrassing were the costume fittings because nothing in stock ever fit me. All my costumes had to be made specially, or I had to buy the special clothes.

As the season went on, I played and worked hard. I remember one day asking the managing director, Judy Gentry, why they had hired me. She said that they had seen potential in me.

My fellow intern, Coleman Ziegen, also encouraged me. He showed me a picture of himself when he weighed more than 325 pounds. He was huge, and I wouldn't have guessed it was the same person. Through dealing with his feelings and eating healthy vegetarian meals, he had become a lean leading man. I learned that people loved me but that my size was getting in the way of my ambitions.

A Matter of Life and Death

On January 17, 1996, I got a dose of reality at my doctor's office, where I was having my annual physical. I knew I was overweight. I'd been trying to lose weight since college, but I hadn't been successful. I wasn't happy about my size, but I'd gotten used to it and learned to rationalize it away.

I was able to do this because I was successful in other areas of my life, such as my career and the theater. Some guys wanted to date me, and I was doing some local plus-size mall modeling. I even entered a magazine print model contest and was selected as the winner for the state of Michigan. How many times had I heard, "You have a great personality and a pretty face"? This helped reinforce that I was okay and not really fat. But as the weight kept piling on, it became harder and harder for me to ignore that I was wearing the largest size in the store.

I was close to 330 pounds at the time. At one point, my weight had been even higher—to the point where the bathroom scale couldn't register it. Walking up a flight of stairs left me so winded that I had to stop at the top to catch my breath.

On vacation with friends during the summer of 1995, I signed up to go horseback riding. When we arrived at the barn, there was a sign that said you couldn't ride if you weighed more than 220 pounds. I ended up sitting on the sidelines, embarrassed and depressed.

I went on vacation with some friends and, at size 26W, I was too heavy to even go horseback riding.

My "fat" clothes were getting tighter and tighter at a size 26W. Even the plus-size stores didn't go bigger than that. I had tried every diet at one time or another, including over-the-counter diet pills. I would have used Optifast, like Oprah Winfrey, if I could have afforded it. I was like this schizophrenic yo-yo: I was up, I was down, but I never felt as if I was in control. I would fluctuate as much as ten to forty pounds on this diet roller coaster.

Using Oprah's experience as a guide, I went out and hired a personal trainer. He helped me with strength training and the cardiovascular side of getting fit, but his knowledge of nutrition was limited, so he didn't monitor what I ate. I worked hard, but after every workout I rewarded myself with a Big Mac and a large order of fries.

I lied to my trainer and told him that I was losing weight. I went to the women's locker room to weigh in, knowing he wasn't allowed in there. I stared at the scale, not wanting to face the truth. No weight loss—actually, the scale often showed a weight gain. I told my trainer what he wanted to hear, not the truth. I didn't want to let him down. I couldn't control my weight for me.

It all came to a head that day in the doctor's office. "Judy," he said, "you really need to do something about your weight."

I'd heard it before. People kept telling me I'd feel better if I lost some weight. I didn't want to listen, and I always ended up feeling hurt by the comments.

On my way out, I caught a glimpse of my chart. I could make out only two words, but those two words made my breath catch in my throat: "morbidly obese."

Morbidly, as in *leading to death.*

That's when it hit me. All of a sudden, I was shaky and teary and scared. I had been forced to look into the future, and it didn't look good. That's when I vowed to take control of my life. It wasn't just about weight anymore. It was about my life. I could die. I needed to learn about living, not just being alive.

This was the first time losing weight wasn't simply about fitting into a certain dress or dealing with how other people saw me. It wasn't about putting value on myself based on weight and size. "I've got to find a way to stay away from McDonald's," I told myself. If I didn't seize control of my life right now, it might be too late.

That day, my life changed forever. I made a choice to end the way I was living and to find a new beginning. Since then, I've learned a lot, I've lost 130 pounds over three years, and fitness has again become a source of joy in my life. I'm going to share with you how I did it—how I *am* doing it. This book describes my personal recipe of goal setting, education, enthusiasm, and a fair bit of sweat. It's a recipe guaranteed to result in a healthier life.

The Journey

The journey from the couch to the course took some blood, sweat, and tears. This process is not instant; it takes time. Here are some outtakes from the beginning of my journey to the present.

I watched Oprah's weight loss show on November 22, 1993. I was so moved by her honesty in sharing her struggles. So many times I've felt the same way. She said, "If weight has been an issue for you, today's show will hopefully lead you to win your own battle."

I took notes, but it was amazing how many of her journal entries mirrored mine. I, too, know about hating myself because of the weight. Like Oprah, I know that even though I realize what I am doing to myself, I continue to eat. And also like her, I need to face the truth and find the motivation to change.

NOVEMBER 24, 1993: *What am I afraid of? Failure. What do I want? Approval. I want people to like me. It dawns on me that I am afraid of letting people really get to know me.*

I look back at college photos and realize that I was not fat then. Now I am horrible. I am not happy with my weight. Why is everything about my weight?

Being here, working at the theater, continues to emphasize how I feel about my weight and size. I should be focusing on developing my craft. I want to be pretty and skinny so I can make heads turn and choose whatever part I want.

How can I do this? I know what is necessary, but I'm afraid I don't have the discipline or heart—truth, maybe—to be able to do it. I spend so much time trying to make people like me that I spend no time on myself.

There are no more journal entries in 1993 after this date. I led an active life, but deep down there was a physical self that I could not deny.

JUNE 17, 1994: *I am back in Michigan after working on an acting internship for ten months. I have lost fifteen pounds while at the theater. Now I really need to get more weight off so I can get better roles. I am focused on losing weight to look better. I even found a personal trainer.*

JUNE 20, 1994: *I started with my trainer today. I have even put together my first exercise log to track my workouts and progress. Feeling excited about starting!*

JULY 16, 1994: *I did a 5K walk with my dad this morning. It was in downtown St. Joe along the bluff and lakefront. I walked as fast as I could. I was very winded and my legs were sore, but I tried to keep going. My dad was just behind me and said to keep going. I am moving toward my goal of that marathon just as Oprah did.*

AUGUST 29–SEPTEMBER 4, 1994: *I haven't worked out all week. I really just don't care about this anymore. I am tired and frustrated most of the time.*

OCTOBER 9, 1994: *I went down to South Bend to try running a 5K. I was excited and nervous at the same time. My routine has been pretty out of whack. I finished today feeling timid, hurt, and tired and nursing a sore knee. I had no business being out there this morning.*

NOVEMBER 4, 1994: *Sprained my ankle playing basketball. Ended up in the emergency room for it. Off for five to seven days.*

DECEMBER 5, 1994: *I have been really irregular with working out. I am working a lot and late way too often. I feel so tired and frustrated with everything. And I'm overeating to the max!*

DECEMBER 6, 1994: *Motivation zero.*

DECEMBER 12–18, 1994: *I haven't worked out all week. I am emotionally weak and have no motivation for this anymore.*

DECEMBER 19, 1994: *Renewed and have a new focus. Somewhat sore and no endurance. Focusing on the new year and getting this weight off.*

JANUARY 10–16, 1995: *I haven't done anything. I am continuing to eat and not work out. I don't want to face my trainer anymore. I am giving up. Work is a good excuse not to have to work out. Now I have started a part-time job on the weekends, too.*

FEBRUARY 13, 1995: *I am back at aerobics class occasionally. Feeling okay but overwhelmed.*

MARCH 22, 1995: *My mind and body are depressed.*

APRIL 13, 1995: *Canceled all training sessions for the month. I talked with my trainer, and he said it is good that I am finally looking into a nutritionist.*

From April on, the journal and exercise logs are empty. I had given up. During this time, I gained back some of the weight I'd taken off—sixty pounds.

JANUARY 17, 1996: *It hit me. No longer is my weight about vanity, a perfect dress, or looking a certain way, but about a huge risk to my life. At an annual doctor's appointment, I saw on the checkout sheet that I am morbidly obese. Crushing and shocking at that moment. But I knew it was my moment to make changes—and make them now.*

That's when everything changed for me. My goal was to reclaim my health. I started very slowly. First, I attended a wellness class that taught me a new focus on well-being, not dieting. I joined the health club again. I started with volleyball. I loved the sport, but I knew there were some bad issues there that I needed to come to peace with. I played once a week for a month, slowly getting back into moving.

FEBRUARY 7, 1996: *I went to aerobics class tonight. I am tired but feeling really good. The music is great to keep me going. My body is so out of shape, but I have to keep moving. It helps that the fitness staff is so supportive.*

FEBRUARY 11, 1996: *I went back to aerobics class today. Early Saturday morning classes, but I was jazzed up for sure.*

I set a goal to go to aerobics class three times the following week, then three times the week after that. I was doing great and having fun going to class. The weekly wellness class was really helping, too. I didn't realize that I could take all the pressure off myself by focusing on creating a healthy lifestyle instead of tackling another diet. I finally began dealing with the issue of my weight.

FEBRUARY 24, 1996: *The guy I was dating broke up with me. He says he can't handle my weight anymore. Sure, I am wonderful on the inside, but he is embarrassed at what others say. He tells me of a time when we were out and he overheard some guys making fun of me. He was upset because he thought if they only knew me. But still he doesn't want to see me anymore.*

I shared my hurt and sadness with others. Talk about a first in my life! Rather than turning to food, I turned to friends for comfort. This process of sharing helped, although the rejection was hard.

FEBRUARY 26, 1996: *I had my fitness evaluation today. Yikes! 48.7 percent body fat! I am so bummed out, but I can't stop this time. I quit before. You keep going, Judy! More aerobics classes, walking. Hey, today I even set my sights on a spring 5K. I saw a poster for it as I left the health club today.*

I learned about how to keep a food journal from the wellness class, so I put one together. It complemented my exercise log.

MARCH 7, 1996: *I started taking yoga today. Talk about the body feeling good! I also lifted weights and got in a few games of volleyball.*

MARCH 11, 1996: *I am finally up to jogging a mile on the indoor track. I had such a great day! I feel I am getting stronger with each lap.*

MARCH 17, 1996: *I can't believe it! I jogged for 1.8 miles today! It was excellent. Also, my weight is dropping off so fast. I was told by the fitness staff that the more weight you have to lose, the faster it comes off in the beginning.*

MARCH 27, 1996: *Woke up with very sore throat and fever. I think I am pushing myself too hard too soon. I decided to take the day off.*

MARCH 29, 1996: *Off to California to visit my brother and his family. I got in a run or two while there. My niece asked me, "Aunt Judy, how come you are so fat?" Wow! I looked at her, stunned. My sister-in-law told her that wasn't polite. I said, "Hey, but it is true."*

APRIL 3, 1996: *Up to 2.2 miles of straight jogging! I am getting so close.*

APRIL 12, 1996: *The day before the race. Talk about nervous and excited. I am taking it easy today for sure. I have been running strong and consistently, so I should be ready to do the 5K (3.1 miles).*

APRIL 13, 1996: *Race day. The morning is very cold, rainy, and windy. I end up wearing a sweatshirt because it is one cold spring morning. I wear a sweatshirt that says GOING THE DISTANCE. My mantra: "Keep going!" As we are all waiting inside for the race to start, I notice some of the lean top competitors talking. I try to keep focused on me and my goal to finish today.*

My first race.

The race is trying with the cold temps and winds. I can feel my face turning blue. I start off at a steady pace, just like I have been running. At the one-mile marker, I am getting tired and all the people are way ahead of me. I start to think I can make it all the way. But then I notice as we make a turn around the campus buildings, there is a lake we have to run around. The grass is wet; there is goose poop everywhere. I am doing my best to dodge the goose poop mines. I make the turn around the lake, and the guys say less than a quarter of a mile! I am almost done. Funny what you can do when you aren't thinking about the distance. I finish. Since it is such a small race, I even get a medal for third place in my age group. I come home with a medal! I am so happy that this time around I am really in control of my health.

APRIL 16, 1996: *My sights are still set on a marathon race. So I drove to Chicago to learn about marathon training from Jeff Galloway. It was very motivational. He made the preparation seem as if anyone could do it if they put in the time and training. He even talked about the mental tricks you have to play on the left side of your brain. When he was telling the stories, I thought, "Hey, that happened to me with the goose poop mines!"*

For the next few weekends, I was so focused on my goals of running to get healthy that I did two more 5K events.

APRIL 21, 1996: *I saw a flyer for a triathlon with all the race entries at the YMCA. I started asking around about the event. I figured I had already done two 5Ks, why not build to a 10K and add in some swimming and biking? Most of the fitness staff didn't know about how to train for one. I talked to a woman at the club wearing a T-shirt from the event. I asked her if she had done it, and she said, "No way—that is way too much," although she loved volunteering for it. I asked her about the 1.5-mile swim in the lake. She said, "Last year it was cold, but it isn't 1.5 miles but 1.5K." I asked what is that then. She said, "I think under a mile." Well, there it was. The distance now seemed doable for some strange reason.*

APRIL 30, 1996: *I sent in my entry form for the Schu's International Triathlon in St. Joseph, Michigan, on August 10 in my backyard. I even signed up for a duathlon race in May. I need to keep building up to August.*

I spent the next few weeks continuing to go to aerobics class and running, and I added time on the stationary bike. I even started asking around about coaching. When I found a contact for a coach at the Triathlon Federation, he gave me suggestions for clubs in the larger cities around me. Then I got a copy of *Triathlete* magazine with an ad offering coaching services.

On May 6, I spoke to coach Troy Jacobson about my goals and his services. I told him that I was very overweight and had no background in any of the sports, but I wanted to do this triathlon in August and lose some weight. We spoke for more than an hour about my goals, current fitness level, and expectations. A week later, I received his fitness questionnaire, which would help give him an understanding of my current fitness level.

MAY 19, 1996: *I am in Columbus to do a duathlon—a 5K run, then a 30K bike, then a 5K run. I was so excited to get out there. I had done several*

5Ks, but all my bicycling was on a stationary bike. My friend loaned me his mountain bike for the event. Well, today was a long day. I did the first 5K fine, but cruising along on the bike afterward was very slow. I made it, but when I got off I had no legs. I felt as if I had tree stumps. I managed to push through the 5K barely. I was the second-to-last person to finish.

For the next couple of weeks, I adjusted to living and working in Columbus, Ohio. I found a new health club and a new routine to follow.

June 1, 1996: *This morning, I went to a 10K race. I have been working out really strong while here in Columbus. The thought of the 10K was a bit intimidating. I kept telling myself I could make this distance. All morning, I was trying to be positive, although I had huge butterflies in my stomach. The whole field of runners was upbeat. I finished without walking once. I was so thrilled when I crossed that finish line. One guy I met had done the same duathlon I had done a few weeks before. He said he remembered me from the mountain bike I was riding. After talking to him, I realized that when I go to races, I stand out due to my size and weight.*

June 3, 1996: *I received my first faxed triathlon program from Troy today. I am excited to have the support of his telling me how much and when to train. Up until this point, I have put the running puzzle together. But wow! This shows me how to put together swimming, biking, and running.*

June 4, 1996: *Today I started my first program for training for a triathlon. I did really well on the forty-five-minute bike and was able to handle the thirty-minute run. I have really worked hard this winter and spring to get my body in better shape. I can't believe how great I have been feeling. I swam for the first time today! Yikes! Okay, the swimsuit issue—get over it, Judy. I think this is the hardest part of the sport—getting into the pool at my size. I barely got through the first part of the workout. I had to swim breast and back to keep going.*

JUNE 9, 1996: *Well, Sunday morning in downtown Columbus. I did another 10K road race this morning. Did fine and even had a guy run the last mile in with me. About a quarter through the race, I went by these two guys and a woman running. As I was in front of them, I heard the one guy say, "Hey, are you going to let that fat chick pass you?" Talk about feeling hurt. But I just kept running, and, as a matter of fact, I never saw them again until I cheered for her coming across the finish line. I even walked up to the guy and said, "Hey, I am not bad for a fat chick, am I?" Wow, did he take a step back. He couldn't believe I heard him. He kept apologizing and saying he was just trying to keep her from quitting. I told him it's okay if I kept her motivated not to give up because she was skinny and I wasn't. Well, it proved to me that, no matter what, I can do these races.*

JUNE 14, 1996: *Home for the weekend. I am even going to do this triathlon race at the YMCA. The swim is in the pool.*

JUNE 15, 1996: *Talk about a wild experience! Swimming laps in a pool, then going outside to ride for six miles then run for two miles. I had fun. Troy said it was good to do as it would give me an idea of what transition means. I am slow is what it means.*

JUNE 25, 1996: *Didn't get to work out as scheduled due to having to attend meetings. It was a long day for sure and then dinner with clients. I tried to run late when I got back, but I was too tired.*

JULY 4, 1996: *Fourth of July! Since I am living out of town for work, I decided to do a 5K today. I actually had a personal best this morning. But when I called to tell Troy, I got lectured. He said, "You are following a plan, and straying from it will interfere with your goal of the 10K you have planned in a few weeks and the August triathlon." He said running a 5K every weekend to see results is like stepping on a scale every day and wanting results. It gets frustrating, because I DO want the results. Okay, be patient!*

JULY 8–11, 1996: *In San Diego for client meetings. I was able to get most of my scheduled workouts in. I even rented a bike to ride along the beach. It was a nice change of pace.*

JULY 18, 1996: *Headed home for the weekend. I am doing a 10K and a marathon one-mile swim. I am very nervous because it is my first open-water swim. I think the last time I was in Lake Michigan was when I was a teenager—and then I was just lying out in the sun.*

JULY 20, 1996: *Saturday was a big day because the 10K and swim are part of the Venetian Summer Festival in St. Joseph, Michigan. I did great with the 10K in the morning and then headed over to the swim event later in the day. I saw a lot of familiar faces standing on the beach waiting for the race to start. The swim director was concerned because the water temperature was 67 degrees and the waves were huge. I guess early in the day a town up from us had to cancel their swim race. So they decided wet suits would be allowed, although it was a non–wet suit event. I don't own a wet suit yet.*

I was so scared! A woman—her name is Ty; I met her through her mom earlier this year as part of a mall fashion show—was nice enough to loan me a surfing wet suit. It fit, but I had never, ever worn one before. I got into the cold water, and I thought I was going to choke. The wet suit was pulling on me, the waves were crashing on me, and I kept swimming forward only to get pushed back. After reaching the first marker, I turned back because I was so scared. I couldn't do it. I got back to the beach crying. My mom said, "It's okay. You should have seen all the people who ran in and came right back out." At that moment, I was determined to do what I could to prepare myself for open-water swimming. After all, the Schu's Triathlon was only three weeks away.

For the next several weeks, my exercise log recorded workout after workout. I even came home early from Columbus to have time to get used to the Lake Michigan waters.

JULY 26, 1996: *Went to the doctor because I was getting dizzy in the pool. It turns out I was not eating enough. When he looked at my exercise log and food log, he said, "You have to make sure to eat enough if you are going to be training like this." My first lesson that food is fuel. I took his advice and started to supplement my day with Ensure Light. I was working for the leading liquid nutritional company, so why not try using the product? It made a difference.*

AUGUST 5, 1996: *One week until Schu's. This is the week. I have worked hard this summer to make it to this point. I have kept positive about finishing. Now it's time to put it all together. I have today off.*

AUGUST 9, 1996: *At work my friend and coworker Teri Gersonde fills my office with signs that say SWIM, JUDY, SWIM! BIKE, JUDY, BIKE! RUN, JUDY, RUN! I am so fired up by the support.*

AUGUST 10, 1996: *Scared. Last year, the water temperatures were in the high fifties and they had some problems. This year, as I was heading down from the bluff to the transition area, the radio station there was announcing water temperatures in the low fifties. At least this time I had my own wet suit. But the concern was becoming more real. I tried not to think about it. I focused on the first experience—getting my body marked. Literally. They took a black marker and wrote my race number on my arms and legs.*

In the transition area, I set up my bike and run equipment just like I had read about and practiced. I figured out how not to have to put a bra on in public. Wear it during the swim.

We waited and waited on the beach. The swim start was delayed by an hour. They were trying to figure out what to do since the water temperature was forty-eight degrees! Since this was a U.S. Pro Triathlon Championship race, there HAD to be a swim. After some time, they said wet suits were mandatory and we would swim a shortened course along the shoreline.

I watched as people got in that water to swim and then stood up to jog in the water. It was so cold it felt like putting your foot in a bucket of ice! I decided to swim what I could. I remember my mom and dad walking along the shore spotting me.

About 800 yards later, out of the swim we came. And then on to the bike. It was so cold. I didn't care, though, because I was having fun just being out there. I made the first steep climb, and I don't think I shifted my gears once. I didn't know how—I just bought the bike two weeks before.

I pedaled along feeling free. I was out there!

I got into the transition for the run. I got a high five from Mom and Dad, and off I went.

I was flying high, feeling good. I stayed within myself and just jogged along. It finally hit me when I saw the finish line along the bluff. I started to cry and smile at the same time. I was finally home. I had finally freed myself from the unhealthy fat girl. I couldn't have been happier when I hit that finish line.

AUGUST 17, 1996: *I broke my foot while walking along a sidewalk. I stepped on a spike, and they tell me I'll have to have surgery. In that one moment, it felt like everything I've worked for was all taken away.*

AUGUST 21, 1996: *Surgery. I am so depressed.*

For the next twelve weeks, I didn't bother to fill out an exercise or eating log. I focused on recovering. I did some strength training with a personal trainer, the only thing my doctor said I could do, as long as I didn't put pressure on my foot.

I had an incredible amount of support, as I was working in Columbus on assignment again. My client contact, Marianne, brought me ice and meals daily. Even Angie, whom I worked with, was on ice patrol. I will never forget their taking care of me, getting me to and from surgery and making sure I was okay.

During this time, eating healthy was not a priority. I snacked on junk food while staying home and off my feet. Talk about a lonely and depressing two weeks. One week I was high on finishing my first race, and then I was sidelined for what promised to be months. Somehow I had to refocus on getting healthy.

After two weeks, I was free to go back to the office. I had to learn how to get around all over again. I kept thinking, "Someone with a handicap has to deal with this every day," but still it was hard.

OCTOBER 15, 1996: *Yeah! The cast came off! But now weeks of physical therapy. At least I can get into the pool. This was the best day, because now I can return to what I was doing. I think this break was meant to slow me down.*

DECEMBER 2, 1996: *Back on a track! Today I get to slowly start returning to running, following my doctor's return-to-running plan.*

DECEMBER 3, 1996: *I learned a lesson through all this. Never do I want my health taken away.*

My December exercise entries go on about getting back in the game. I started with a visit to my doctor to set some goals. I had a plan (with less structure) as to what I wanted to do in 1997: Race! Race! Race! No longer was it about reaching a magic number on the scale.

For the 1997 season, I set my sights on several races that I had read about while in a cast—exotic-sounding races like Escape from Alcatraz, the Hood to Coast Relay, and the Vineman Half Ironman. That year, I managed to compete in eight triathlons including two Half Ironman events (a Half Ironman is a 1.2-mile swim, a 56-mile bike ride, and a 13.1-mile run). I made the infamous Escape from Alcatraz in fifty-four-degree water and even joined a team to do the Hood to Coast Relay. I reached all my goals. I kept focused on learning about the sport and getting healthy. More weight came off, but a bit more slowly. All that was important was that my lifestyle had changed for the better.

The 1998 season arrived with new goals and a wonderful new training partner—my boyfriend, Rick. He added joy

Finishing my first triathlon was one of the biggest rushes of my life.

to my life. I had finally learned to love myself for who and what I was. Now I was ready to share that love with someone else.

Rick is my best friend, my soul mate, the love of my life. He also does triathlons with me. I did six races in 1998, including another Half Ironman and a failed attempt at the Hawaii Ironman (a 2.4-mile swim, a 112-mile bike ride, and a marathon). Rick put it in perspective as I walked toward him and my family after I quit the race: "Do you want the Ironman finisher's medal or your weight back?"

At that moment, I knew that no matter how any race goes, no matter what comments anyone makes, I have something no one can give to me or take away from me: my health and a healthy lifestyle. I carried this thought with me into the 1999 season of triathlons. The biggest victory of the year was my completion of the Hawaii Ironman, which is also the greatest personal achievement in my life.

The Races

Often I am asked, "Why do you do these races? What is the point if you never win?"

Racing for me is the difference between working toward a concrete goal and working out for some abstract reason. We all know the benefits of exercise in decreasing the risks of many diseases. Adding regular exercise to my lifestyle made a huge difference in my mental and physical well-being. But preparing for and participating in a race brought new challenges and a sense of accomplishment. To finish a race, I had to do certain things right, such as staying focused on a goal, exercising consistently, eating right, drinking enough water, and getting enough sleep—basically, taking care of myself and treating my body right.

I didn't wake up one morning and say, "Let's do triathlons." I try to explain to people that the struggle with weight is long term and has many ups and downs. My weight was all-consuming. I had tried all the diets out there. I had even hired a trainer and tried running. Finally, I learned how to deal with the ups and downs and keep going every day. My goals were not centered on losing weight and looking beautiful. Instead, I learned to care about health and fitness. I learned to care about *me.*

How I Became the Chub Club Coach

Many people ask me how I became the Chub Club coach. Was I Rosie O'Donnell's friend? Nope. I met Rosie as a guest on her show in 1998.

In 1996, I started walking, which eventually led to running. I learned everything I could about nutrition, health, and fitness. I began changing what, when, how, and why I ate. I started keeping a training log. I joined a health club and found a coach. I raced in my first 5K, then set my sights on running a 10K. I started cross-training and decided to do a triathlon. After the triathlon, I just kept aiming for higher goals. I wanted to see how far I could go. I went on to train for and run my first marathon in January 1998 and received a spot for the Hawaii Ironman Triathlon in the fall of that year.

As a result of my new lifestyle, I lost 130 pounds. I went from doughnut junkie to healthy and fit. It didn't happen overnight, but it did happen. I worked hard, and I kept a positive attitude.

Paula Newby-Fraser was an inspiration to me. Not only was she the top female endurance athlete, having won the Hawaii Ironman an unprecedented eight times, but she'd also had to deal with weight gain after college when she settled into a nine-to-five job. A friend had urged her to start running to lose the extra weight. She helped me believe that I could be successful in the triathlon, too.

As I was training for the Hawaii Ironman, I got a call from the public relations firm that handles the race, Alan-Taylor Communications. The firm sends out media releases on all the competitors before the event. Keith Fernbach called and said, "Guess whose TV show you are going on."

I said, "Rosie's?" He said yes, and I started to scream and jump up and down.

"Before you get too excited," he said, "you have to do a preview interview to see if you can actually go on the show." He explained that my biography had been submitted to the producers of the show. They were interested in my story—how I had lost weight, gotten control of my health, and gotten fit enough to attempt one of the world's toughest endurance events.

The next day, I received a call from Terence Noonan, the show's human interest producer. I think his first question was, "Do you watch the show?" I told him that since I worked during the day, I usually didn't get to see it. But I said that

I had seen all of Rosie's movies. We spoke about my interests and hobbies, how I had lost the weight, and why I wanted to do the Ironman.

A few days later, I found out that I was going on the show for sure. I was floored. I didn't tell anyone except my parents and boyfriend until the date was set. Then it became big news to share with everyone.

I went to New York in September to tape the show. At that time, Rosie's show was taped live and shown later. The show I was on was going to air on September 14, 1998. It was so wild to actually fly to New York and do the show. Terence explained the whole process, but I still had no idea what to expect. The advice my boyfriend gave me was just to be myself. I wasn't nervous because everyone else was nervous for me. When I finally made my entrance onto that stage, I thought, "This is it! I'm here!"

I think it finally dawned on me that I was really on television when I sat down and looked at Rosie sitting behind the desk. I shared my story and why I wanted to do the Ironman. It was an awesome opportunity to share my message about getting healthy not for a quick fix, to reach a certain size, or for vanity, but for a better life. It was liberating to talk about my journey from fat to fit.

Rosie gave me some zinc to wear on my nose during the Ironman. She said she was going to follow the race and have me back to talk about the experience.

When I didn't finish the Hawaii Ironman, I figured that she wouldn't want me back on. But I got a call the next day while I was still in Hawaii. The show wanted me back anyhow. I was shocked. I thought, "I didn't finish! Why would they want to hear about that?"

On October 14, just before I made my second appearance on the show, Terence told me, "We didn't care whether you finished the race. What we care about is you and what you did to get there. That's real life."

This appearance was more than I ever expected. Rosie and I chatted about the Ironman, reviewed footage from the event, and joked about her doing a team triathlon with Tom Cruise and me. Then she surprised me with the Broadway singer Robert Cuccioli, who sang my motivational song, "This Is the Moment," from *Jekyll and Hyde*. I couldn't believe that I was hearing in person the song that had inspired me all year long.

Afterward, I went back to Michigan and my job. In mid-December, I received a call from the show saying that they were interested in having me come in once a month to share a motivation or fitness tip. I was thrilled. A few days later, I got from a call from Terence saying that plans had changed and I wouldn't be coming in once a month. Instead, they had decided they were going to start Rosie's Chub Club, and they wanted me to move to New York to be the Chub Club coach.

I quit my job of eight years at a marketing/advertising firm, packed up, and moved to New York. Very soon after, I started working with the show as Chub Club coach.

We launched Rosie's Chub Club on January 4, 1999. There was a huge response. We have more than 300,000 members now, all eating less and moving more, getting healthy and reaching for a better life.

It's an honor to be part of this community of men and women whom I relate to and who are seeking a better life. Here's a success story that exemplifies why I do what I do.

Success Story: Linda

Hi Judy,

I'm sure this has happened 100 times or more to you since last year but I need to pass on some words from a great fan of yours here in Hawaii.

I was sitting waiting at the Kaiser Pharmacy (I have asthma) and the lady next to me was wearing a shirt with a Hawaiian phrase that talked about "Ka Makani Apa'apa'a." The English translation was "You will have freedom and peace with the great wind Apa'apa'a." Now, you and I both know about the Mumuku winds in Waikoloa so I wanted to know which winds brought peace. Evidently these are the winds through Hawi. (I would not call them peaceful AT ALL!)

Anyway, from there we started talking and when I mentioned I was doing the race, she started asking about my swimming, etc. She then asked if I saw the girl (you) on the Ironman coverage on the NBC show last year and how you changed her life. Linda (this is the lady I was talking to) lost her twin sister two years ago and went from 125 to 258 pounds in one year. She said she was miserable about everything (she had lots of life's ailments, too). So when she saw your interview on the Ironman show she (1) wanted to kick the TV when she heard your story about people saying, "You're not going to let a fat chick beat you?!" and (2) decided she could change her life, too!

She is swimming and just started running. She has lost 70 pounds. Her goal is to do the Tinman (Olympic distance) triathlon on Oahu in July 2001—all inspired because of you!

As I left, she said, "Please tell Judy she has a big fan in Hawaii named Linda and I'll be wearing this red shirt at the turnaround for her this year. And give her this for me." With that, she gave me one of the greatest hugs! So now I send it to you. And a huge Mahalo for encouraging so many of us non-petite athletes out there!

Hope your week back at work has been somewhat calm and your training better and better. I have had a tough training week and have a 5:30 hour bike and 40 minute run on Saturday. Sunday has a 1 hour bike and 2:30 hour run! Oh, yeah, sleep, eat, family, shop somewhere in there, too! I must say, though, I am more energized than ever. Even my husband has noticed a new excitement for training. "About time," he says!

Have a super training weekend and stay safe and healthy!

Karen

CHAPTER 2

Sixteen Steps for Getting Ready to Get into the Game

Your thoughts determine your actions. Your actions determine your habits. Your habits determine your character. And your character gives birth to your destiny.

—UNKNOWN

The process of making changes in your life is just that—a process. When faced with the opportunity to make positive changes in your life, it helps to give some thought to developing a strategy to make those changes happen. Like everyone who wants to improve his or her health, there are two areas that I had to focus on changing when I made a decision to get healthy: exercise and diet.

I looked at my life as a teeter-totter, and my job was to stop the bouncing up and down and create a balance. I'm not talking only about the weight highs and lows. I'm also talking about the mental ups and downs. For me, balance meant not only improving the physical but also developing a spiritual and mental self. You might see this as heart, body, and mind. I had known the many ups and downs of dieting. I had to focus my attention inward to get myself in balance.

I even came up with a motto, "Finding It My Way." Then I took a few steps

Mini-goals: that's what each day is for me. Goal number one: eating right. Goal number two: getting out the door to exercise. Goal number three: deciding each day is going to be a great day.

Lauri Levenfeld, Zoom Photography, California

toward making changes. Those changes took time, but I took it step by step. You can "find it your way" by following these practical steps.

Finding Your Way

1 **Become aware.** I had to become aware of where I came from, then figure out where I needed to go. This meant taking a good, honest look at myself—the things I did and why I did them, both positive and negative. What was working in my life and what was not?

I started this process by taking time to write and reflect on how I was going to make some changes in my life. One of the first things I did was write down some of the things that I needed to work and focus on. You don't have to write a lot—sometimes just a few words will say all you need to say. I jotted down a quick list that included the following:

- Do it for *me.*
- Admit fears.
- Concentrate on the small steps.
- Surround myself with supportive people.
- Admit it's okay to slip.
- Self-care is not being selfish.
- Share vulnerability.
- Be committed.
- Trust myself and others.

- Add structure to my life.
- Focus on the positive.
- Be responsible to myself.
- Forgive myself.

From there, I wrote a list of things to do.
- Running
- Weight training
- Doing new things
- Playing volleyball
- Taking a wellness class
- Going to church
- Reading motivational books
- Eating for me
- Creating a new lifestyle of my own

I remember one time I wrote down more than three hundred things that I wanted to accomplish in my life. I wrote down everything I ever thought I might want to do—from traveling and attending a Broadway show to flossing and not cutting myself down. I still have that list, and I look at it every once in a while to keep me focused on new goals.

If you have a minute, start making of list of things you want to accomplish in life—no matter how far out of reach they seem to be. After all, without a dream, your spirit will die.

2 **Review what got you to this point.** This can be tough to admit, but I believe I always knew what I needed to change in my life; I just had to take the time to face it head-on. Before you can make any changes, you have to learn to accept yourself for who you are. This is the most crucial step.

Talking to close friends and family—and listening to what they have to say, even if you don't want to hear it—may give you a clearer perspective on your life. Try to talk to people who care about you and are supportive. Bottom line: I couldn't do it alone.

I talked to a close friend and coworker, Rob Martin—who is one of the most outgoing and goal-oriented people I have ever met—about what things he thought I should change about myself. He never said, "Lose weight." He did say I needed a consistent, positive attitude. He said I should work more on it. He told me that it is so easy to get up each morning and be negative but that it takes work to be positive. He gave me an immediate example of my negativity: I had started our conversation that day by saying, "I'm in a good mood, but it won't last long." Negativity was a real crutch for me, enabling my eating habits and poor fitness: "I can't go to a gym because I'm too big."

Rob told me to refuse to allow the environment around me to affect my attitude, to control what I can and let the rest go. That's a tall order. My boss would rail me for whatever was bothering him that day, and I would take it in and then eat myself through it, rather than confronting him with how he vented his frustrations on me or accepting that the problem was his, not mine.

Rob also told me to lighten up, that I needed to have more fun, enjoy the present moment, and be a bit more spontaneous. Everything—down to when I brushed my teeth—was planned. He said that if I was stressed so much by others and by planning for the future, there would be no time to enjoy me. Essentially, I had to be with myself twenty-four hours a day.

I found that writing in a journal helped me work through my thoughts and deal with the issues of the day. I could see myself on the page.

3 **Set goals.** Don't take a cookie-cutter approach to this process. Your goals are not the same as mine or anyone else's. Your situation is not the same as anyone else's. Don't even imagine that anyone else's plan for reaching his or her goals is going to be the same as yours. Give yourself some leeway.

The ideas presented here are meant as a guide, not as a set of hard-and-fast rules. Pick and choose the ones that appeal to you, then use them to create a structure that works for you and makes you happy.

A goal isn't a goal until you put it down on paper, say it out loud, tell others about it, learn it by heart. Make it into a poster or sampler, or just write it on a piece of paper and tape it to your bathroom mirror, your dashboard, or your refrigerator door—someplace where you will see it every day.

4 **Be realistic.** That doesn't mean you shouldn't have big goals. It does mean you should give yourself the time and resources you need to reach them. Set yourself up for success, not failure. In 1992, I wrote, "I am going to lose forty pounds by the end of the summer and, if I keep going, one hundred pounds by Christmas." Wow! That was a lot of weight to lose in less than six months. Not realistic—and not healthy. Try not to think in terms of pounds lost but rather in terms of health gained.

Visit a Doctor

Okay, you've heard this a million times: you really need a doctor's assessment of your health and fitness. Doctors can take tests to determine things such as blood pressure, cholesterol, heart and thyroid condition, and more. Talk to your doctor about your plans for a new lifestyle. He or she may set limits on your activities or make suggestions about the best kinds of exercise for you. But don't rely on a doctor for nutritional and weight-loss advice unless he or she is experienced in this area.

A coworker went to her doctor because she thought she was gaining too much weight and didn't know why. She had a thyroid test, which came back negative. The doctor told her to eat no more than a thousand calories a day, and she would lose weight. He offered no support or education as to what she should do, just slapped her with a calorie-counting diet plan. She later admitted to me that she *did* know why she was gaining so much: she was eating fast food all the time, and whenever she was stressed at work, she went to the candy machine. She made a change in her life. She quit her job after years of using food to deal with the stress. She has lost weight and is really getting control of her life now.

5 **Make it personal.** Your mother may have goals for you, but that's her problem. Be honest about what *you* want. I tried to follow the Oprah way of going after a marathon. I was going after her dreams and goals, doing it her way, not mine. When I started doing the exercises I liked, I was led to doing triathlons.

Triathlons encompass several exercises, they are social, and they required a lot of learning, which kept me interested day in and day out.

Don't let your goal be dependent on someone else. Their failure then becomes your failure, your excuse.

6 **Set a time frame.** A deadline is always a good motivator. Do a little research. Find out how long it took other people to reach the same goal. Sit down with a calendar and plot out steps along the way. When I decided to do a 5K, I reviewed a lot of training programs to find one that matched my goals, my fitness level, and the time I had available to train. I read magazine articles by running experts that gave advice on training to help me establish when I could realistically expect to be ready.

7 **Set little goals that lead to bigger goals.** Small steps will take you to the end of the road just as big steps will—and do it a lot easier. You don't go from the couch to the finish line overnight. And if you try, you risk frustration, burnout, and injury. When I decided to do a 5K, my first step was to see how far I could walk. Then I set up a plan to walk three times that week. Each time I walked, I went a little farther, building on each success, minute by minute.

Consider a Nutritionist

One of the best things I did was attend a wellness class taught by a nutritionist. This was the first time that I focused on wellness, not just a diet plan. To find a registered dietitian in your area, check the American Dietetic Association website at www.eatright.org, or call (800) 366-1655.

8 **Share your goals and hopes with others.** Tell everyone, "I'm going to run a 5K next September" (or whatever your goal is). People can't help you unless they know what you're trying to do, and you'll be surprised at the help and support you get. Moreover, we all make promises to ourselves, but when we tell someone else, we become accountable.

9 **Figure out what you need to reach your goal, then go out and get it.** Seek out information, support, and people who can direct and guide you. Take a look around your community to find programs, health clubs, and wellness groups that can help you. In the Resources section, I list some websites that can help, too.

10 **Visualize it.** I learned that if I saw myself as successful, I would be successful. It's a mental game of imagining what you want to do, seeing yourself doing it, feeling how it feels to have done it—then trying it in real life.

11 **Easy does it, but do it.** You can spend a lot of time thinking about the changes you want to make. Heck, you can spend so much time thinking about it that you never do anything. Set a time limit for this step. There are just two rules to follow: no negative thinking ("I can't do that") and no procrastination. Get clear on what you want to do, then do it.

It takes courage and support to go after any goal. The key is to take steps forward—even if your goal is to buy a pair of sneakers so that you can join a gym. You just have to keep working toward your goal. You may have to try different routes until you find one that clicks for you—something you enjoy, something fun, something that you'll stick with until you get where you want to go. For instance, I tried the personal trainer route and didn't find complete success because I was focusing only on losing weight and the physical aspects of health. I also tried structured diets time and again, but I always failed because I didn't have a realistic outlook. Then I started walking and found that it got me moving without adding too much stress to my body. Later I started playing volleyball at the health club. It's easier if you approach your goal one small step at a time, celebrate each step you take, and move on to the next one.

12 **Make it yours.** Here is where I finally started to take responsibility for what I had done and what I was doing to make positive changes in my life. For example, I kept my exercise log at hand so that I could continue to track and record my progress. I noted all the positive changes I experienced. By setting goals and plans I had begun to make the process mine. Now, by keeping tabs on my progress, I became accountable only to myself.

13 **Track your goals and progress.** When you set a goal, make sure there's a way to measure your progress and a way to tell when you've reached it. This means make it concrete, such as "I will walk three miles by January 1" or "I will attend a masters swim class twice a week for the next six months." I use an exercise log to record my schedule for each week, then I write in what I did and comment on each day. On those days when I feel as if I'm getting nowhere, I look back over my log, and I get a big boost from seeing how much progress I've made and how I'm building a foundation of health and fitness.

14 **Reward yourself each time you reach a goal.** Make sure it's a positive reward, not a negative one. Get out of the habit of using food as a reward. Do something good for yourself—a manicure or pedicure, a massage, a new outfit, a long-distance call to Mom. One of my friends got new skis when she completed her first race. Hey, why not? Having something to look forward to can keep you moving toward your goal. Remember, rather than celebrating your success with food or a day off, do something that brings you closer to your goal.

15 **Keep your goals current.** Your goals may change. That's okay; it just means you're getting in touch with what you really want. You may not be making much progress toward your goals, which means you need to try another direction or deal with an obstacle you hadn't anticipated. Set new goals as soon as you reach your old ones, so you're always looking ahead, working for something positive in your life.

When you've reached a goal, take a look at your log or journal. Try to spot the problems you had and come up with ways to avoid them next time around. I found that certain patterns developed when I missed a workout, so I started planning for those times. If I had a meeting scheduled for late in the day, there was a chance it would run over into my aerobics class. Knowing this had happened in the past, I would plan a morning workout on days I had late meetings scheduled. Dealing with potential problems ahead of time keeps you from getting off track.

16 **Live it.** It's that simple—and that hard. This is the part that takes patience and commitment to yourself and your goals. You can spend all the time in the world talking and writing about what you want to do, but there comes a time when you have to take action. There are ups and downs on the path of realizing your goal to get healthy. Take the time to learn from this journey. You will experience so much by actually living out your dreams.

A Final Thought: Be Proactive

The hardest part of making healthy lifestyle changes could be making yourself talk to others. Surround yourself with supportive people who are like-minded in terms of reaching for goals and pursuing a healthy lifestyle. I have a supportive family and boyfriend. If you don't have people in your life who are good for you, get out and meet some. Talk to people at your health club. Talk to people you see when you're out walking. Be friendly, be open about your goals, and don't be afraid to ask for help. That's what the Chub Club is all about—providing a supportive community.

Let the people in your life help. I found that I was not alone with my weight and health issues. I sat in a wellness class with thirty other women trying to get control of some of their unhealthy habits. I also talked to a nutritionist. I found a coach. I started reading books. I started making small changes and made sure to share them with those close to me. I found that many people are available to help, but first you need to learn how to help yourself. That is where being proactive about your health comes into play. You have to make it happen.

We all know what we need to do, but it takes will, determination, and even courage to face yourself and others and to begin to make changes. Remember that you are not alone.

CHAPTER 3

Make Your Life a Fit Experience

You have to work hard and pay the price to be what you want to be.

—JOE GIBBS

The first way you can become a healthier person is to move more. At first, it can be very simple. Fitness opportunities are everywhere.

Walk to do some errands instead of driving. Mow the lawn with a push mower. Use a shovel instead of a snowblower. Rather than take the subway to your final stop, get off and walk the last ten blocks. Take the stairs instead of the elevator. Walk the long way to someone's office. When sitting at your desk all day, stop every hour to stretch or march in place. Join company-sponsored teams such as softball, bowling, golf, volleyball, or basketball. Look for alternatives to being sedentary.

A friend of mine started an aerobics class at the office during lunch hour. She would bring in an exercise video, and a small group would get together in a conference room to exercise. Everyone would bring a brown-bag lunch, so once they were done moving and grooving, they would eat together. It was a great time to share healthy tips and recipes, too.

I know you are thinking, "I can't do that. I'll get all sweaty." Well, everyone brought plenty of deodorant, towels, and misting solutions to absorb their sweat. Fans at their desks helped keep them cool after the workout. The advantage was that they didn't have to go to the gym before or after work.

Take a look at your environment. Notice how convenience is making you lazy. We've all gotten used to moving very little during the day. As society continues to expand, so do our bottoms. We have to make an effort to be more active and physical. It can be as simple as getting up to change the TV channel instead of using the remote control.

It's time for you to be creative about getting more active each day. If you find yourself saying you are too busy to exercise, take a look at your priorities. Take charge of your life so that you include not only the day-to-day tasks you must complete but also something that is good for your mind, spirit, and body.

For your well-being, fitness has to be part of your life. It doesn't have to be perfectly structured, but it does have to be something you will enjoy doing every day as part of your regular routine.

Fitness Options

With a few basic fitness items, I found that I could get in a thirty-minute workout no matter what my schedule was for the day. Planning ahead and including exercise as a top priority in your schedule is the best thing to do. Get up thirty minutes earlier, and you can do your exercise before the day gets eaten up with errands, work, appointments, meetings, picking up the kids, and such.

One of the things I did was invest in a set of resistance bands for toning and strength training. It helps to get a set that comes with an instructional video so that you can learn the exercises and follow a routine. Resistance bands are easy to have at home because they take up no space, and they are easy to pack and use when traveling. If you like, you can invest in free weights or dumbbells. Any of these items can give you a good overall body-toning and strength-training workout right in your home. Also check out fitness videos for at-home strength routines.

Exercise equipment for the home, such as a treadmill, stationary bike, or stair stepper, requires a much bigger commitment financially and fitness-wise. It is wise to start slowly. Once you get into a routine, then you can consider buying some home equipment. By the way, these items are meant for exercise—not for hanging clothes on and taking up space.

When traveling on business, I always made it a point to book a hotel that had some type of fitness area. Mind you, all hotels don't have *great* fitness areas, but if they have any cardio machines at all, you can get some exercise in. If all else fails, you can walk outside, walk the hallways, or even walk up and down the stairs.

Cardio Routines

For starters, here are some no-cost cardiovascular exercises you can do to get moving more whether you're at home or in a hotel room.

Walking or jogging is by far the cheapest form of exercise. You can do it pretty much anytime, anywhere. All you need is a good pair of shoes (see page 48).

For those of you working at larger corporations, outdoor walking paths and indoor corridors might be available for walking during breaks or your lunch hour. No one said the time to exercise has to be perfectly structured. The best time to exercise is whenever you can get it in. If your company is large enough to have a fitness facility on location, you can exercise before work, during lunch, or after work at your convenience.

Let's say you have no access to a health club, exercise equipment, or even a sidewalk to walk on. What can you do?

Remember being a kid and jumping around like crazy doing jumping jacks, marching in place, swinging, and twisting? Guess what? That's a cardio routine, and you don't have to be a kid to do it.

Try exercises such as jumping jacks, marching in place, jogging in place, high-knee jogging, stair stepping, lunges, toe touches, push-ups, sit-ups, bench dips, leg raises, and leg lifts. Do each of these activities for about thirty to sixty seconds. Build up until you can go through your whole routine two or three times. As you improve your cardio capabilities add dumbbells for more resistance. Dumbbells are designed to provide a balanced weight, but anything you can safely hold or tie on that won't swing or throw you off balance will increase the amount of work your muscles and heart must do.

If all else fails, put on your favorite music and dance. The key is to move and increase your heart rate.

Find Your First Activity

So you are taking the stairs instead of the elevator, parking at the far end of the lot, and trying to put a little more energy into everything you do. You're already moving more, and now it's time to set up a regular exercise routine. Here's how to do it.

1 **Read about different activities.** Look through fitness magazines for features on various activities. Stop by the bookstore and library to read about exercise options to help you find an activity that you are interested in. There is a book on pretty much any sport you can think of—and a lot of sports activities you've never even heard about. Doing a little research will give you an idea of the time required for each activity, various techniques and exercise plans, and the details that will make doing the activity fun and informed.

2 **Pick things you think you might enjoy.** Take time to think back to any activity you have enjoyed in the past, seen on TV, read about, or even heard a friend or coworker talk about. There are a huge number of exercise options—from taking classes to heading outside for a walk—to get you moving in the right direction. The key is finding one or more that you will be able to stick with. The key to *that* is finding one that's fun and that you'll look forward to doing. I started out playing my old favorite, volleyball, a couple of times a week. It made me feel so good that I started walking, joined a health club, and kept going from there.

3 **Do you want to be inside or outside?** If you enjoy the outdoors, make sure you include a hefty dose of outdoor exercise to balance your indoor training at a health club or at home. This is particularly important for those who work in an office. Running and bicycling satisfied my need to be outside. The only time I don't head outside for running is in extremely cold temperatures or icy conditions. I've learned how to dress smart and layer, so I can run in pretty much any weather.

I can't take more than thirty minutes on a treadmill without feeling like a hamster. That's me. I know a lot of people who like the consistency and convenience of indoor workouts. And it's tough to watch TV or follow a workout video outdoors.

4 **Don't be afraid to try something you haven't tried before.** It's easy to say "I can't do that," "I'm scared to do that," or "I'm not the right size for that activity." Don't limit your choices or hold yourself back from doing an exercise or participating in a sport that interests you. Part of developing a love for exercise is the adventure and challenge of trying new things. And if that means rock climbing, go for it!

5 **Check if the sport you're interested in has an association.** Most major, and many minor, exercise activities have a governing association that you can write to or call or a website you can log on to. This is the easiest way to learn more about how to participate and where to find coaches or classes, as well as to find information on recommended equipment, basic techniques, training plans, races, and more.

6 **Do you want to compete?** If your goal includes a need to compete in a sport, make sure the exercise you pick has *local* competitive events. Most sports—from walking and running to swimming, cycling, karate, and rock climbing—offer competitive opportunities. Setting your sights on a race or other competition is more likely to keep you going, as you have something to plan and shoot for.

7 **See what your friends are doing.** Ask around to find out what your friends and coworkers are into. Ask them questions such as why they do it, how much time is required to learn it, and whether they would be willing to allow you to participate with them. This way, you instantly start building a support group of like-minded people to keep you going. Working out with a group guarantees working out more consistently.

8 **Get the right equipment.** If you're on a tight budget, stay away from exercises and sports that require a lot of equipment. If you need more than just a good pair of shoes, try starting out with used equipment or even rentals. That can give you the opportunity to try out a sport or exercise without making a huge investment. If you decide you love the sport and you are sure you want to continue, you can get your own equipment. Ask others involved in the sport for advice on where and what to buy.

I'll run from tree to tree or post to post. I'll break the run into little pieces, little power dots that make each step exciting.

Lauri Levenfeld, Zoom Photography, California

9 **Check out the learning curve.** Some sports take longer to learn than others. Walking is pretty easy—just make sure your shoes offer enough support and be aware of your posture. Walk tall. A sport such as rock climbing is going to take some professional instruction. Team sports require finding at least one team to play on and one to play against, as well as finding time for regular practice. This is where patience comes in. If you're easily frustrated, look for a sport with a short learning curve, one that requires few specific skills, such as walking or running. If you enjoy learning new things and challenging your mind as well as your body, a sport with a long learning curve, such as rock climbing or snowboarding, will keep you from getting bored. If you do well in a very social environment, team sports are good, or look for a sport that lends itself to group workouts, such as running, walking, cycling, or masters swimming.

10 **Do you want instruction or coaching?** Pretty much any exercise or sport has instruction or coaching available to get you started. It's great to have some supervision when you're starting out with a new activity—or even when you're going back to a favorite sport after a long time. A class or coach can give you the basics, help you get the most out of your exercise, and keep you from getting injured. Having to make it to class or meet with your coach also will help keep your commitment alive. Don't be embarrassed—you're not supposed to be great at first. You're there to learn, to get better. So look around for classes at community centers or individuals who might teach or coach your sport. Local YMCAs and colleges often offer coaches and trainers at no extra cost.

11 **Do you need a classroom environment?** If you want the social environment of a classroom, check out local health clubs, the YMCA or YWCA, and community centers for a list of scheduled classes. You can take part in activities such as aerobics, yoga, dance, water aerobics, kickboxing, spinning, and more with an instant support group. The scheduled times provide consistency, you'll get great instruction, and you'll meet new people with similar interests.

12 **What are your goals for an exercise or sport?** Take a look at your goals and make sure the exercise or sport you choose will help you reach them. I chose to participate in triathlons when I recognized that I needed to do cross-training, since I get bored easily with one activity. The triathlon was perfect for me because two of the sports—swimming and cycling—are non-weight-bearing and thus a bit easier on the joints.

13 **Create a time to do this activity.** At first, you may schedule only fifteen minutes three times a week to walk, but it's essential that you begin to make this activity as much a part of your daily routine as showering or brushing your teeth.

No matter what exercise or sport you want to participate in, just try it. If it doesn't meet your needs or expectations, move on to something else. There's so much out there to get you moving and keep you moving. You just have to make the decision to get started. Where you go from there will be your own personal adventure.

Success Story: Theresa

At thirty-eight years old and tipping the scales at 198 with her cholesterol level out of control, Theresa was faced with a decision that could affect her health forever. She did not want to take medication, so she decided to lower her health risks and her cholesterol by changing her eating habits and exercising. "I had dealt with the ups and downs of weight for over eight years," she says. "I had never tried dieting because you diet for so long, then afterward you just gain all the weight back. So I knew dieting was not for me. I knew I had to get active again."

One of the first changes Theresa made was cutting out soda and sweets. Now she reaches for a bottle of water rather than a can of soda.

Theresa is married and has two boys, ages thirteen and eleven, who keep her very busy. She also works full-time as a real estate transfer deputy.

"When you have a family, it is hard to take time for yourself," Theresa says. "Now that my children are older, I can find time. But you really should take time out for yourself, no matter what.

"My brother and his girlfriend motivated me to get into a consistent fitness routine. Through checking out some of the activities they were doing, I went about choosing what exercises were right for me."

Currently, Theresa has a fitness routine that includes kickboxing and spinning at the YMCA. She also rides her mountain bike off-road and on-road with her sons. "My sons even go hiking and walking with me now," Theresa says. "It is a great time to spend talking and sharing with them."

Theresa has lost twenty-eight pounds so far. Her cholesterol level has dropped to normal, so she doesn't have to take any medication. She is now in control of her health. Her goals are to put more miles on her bike by entering races and to continue to lose weight.

"No matter how hard exercising may be at first, the reward down the road is such a great feeling," she says. "I have noticed that I have more energy that lasts all day. My body has toned up, and I have dropped three dress sizes. Sure, I receive many compliments on my weight loss. But now I try to motivate others, as I was motivated, to exercise. If they see what I have accomplished so far, maybe they too can believe that a mom with a busy family can find time to take care of herself."

Theresa is committed to this active lifestyle and a focus on eating right because it keeps her in control of her health, without medication. "I love it!" she says. "Burn, baby, burn!"

CHAPTER 4

Finding a Way to Move More That's Right for You

You must do the thing you think you cannot do.
—ELEANOR ROOSEVELT

Here's a short list of activities that I've done to help me move more.

Walking

Walking is one of the best exercises to help get you moving. It is a weight-bearing exercise, so it can help prevent osteoporosis. It is also one of the cheapest and easiest exercises you can do. All that is required is walking shoes and the commitment to head out the door. Sometimes you have to be creative if the weather keeps you inside. During the winter, my dad gets to the office early and takes a twenty- or thirty-minute walk around the building. I have seen many mall walkers out getting their exercise—which also gives them a chance to do some window-shopping.

Walking helps strengthen your hamstrings, quadriceps, and hips. It took a lot for me to make it around the block the first time out. I set a goal of making it to the corner, the next telephone pole, or a certain house, each time setting the goal just a little farther down the street. It really helps to have landmarks to keep you moving forward.

> **Basic equipment:** You, walking shoes, a hat, water, and sunscreen. If you're walking outdoors after dark, you also need reflective clothing, a flashlight, a buddy, and a cell phone.
>
> **Extra equipment to jazz up your workout:** A digital step counter, hand weights, and special walking shorts and shirts.
>
> **Location:** Outside on an outdoor track, along trails, or in your neighborhood. Inside on a treadmill, on an indoor track, or in a mall.
>
> **Cost:** Minimal. The key is to invest in good-quality walking shoes.
>
> **How to start:** Make a commitment to yourself. Schedule your time to walk just like any other appointment. Make sure to lay out your shoes and clothing so you don't forget and you can get going quickly. Remember to warm up and walk with purpose and good posture. Really move that body forward by keeping your arms strong and swinging at your sides.
>
> **Research:** I recommend *Jaywalking* by Jay Ciniglio, an awesome book on the total walking experience.

Road Runner Sports' Guide to Finding the Shoe That Fits

When you walk, your foot starts by turning outward and becoming rigid to prepare for the force of impact. That's why most runners land on the outside of the heel. Normally, after the initial impact, the foot loosens up and rolls inward; this is called *pronation*.

Pronation allows the foot and body to adapt to varying surfaces and to absorb shock. After it pronates, the foot becomes rigid again as your body weight is transferred over the ball of the foot so that it can toe-off.

There are three basic types of pronation. Neutral pronation is described above. Over-pronation occurs when the foot rolls in too much. Under-pronation occurs when the foot is too stiff and does not roll in enough. The correct shoe can take care of potential problems caused by over-pronation and under-pronation. The wrong shoes can lead to major, chronic injuries.

The Right Category for Your Foot

Once you know how your foot moves when running, you can determine the category of running shoes you should look for.

Flat-footed runners need a shoe that keeps the foot from rolling too far. These shoes are called *motion control shoes* because they are built with a wide base of support and are generally stiff.

Medium-arched runners need a shoe that allows the foot to roll naturally. Because of the force of impact while running, you still need to control the tendency of the foot to roll too much. Look for *stable shoes* that have a medial (under your heel or arch) post.

Stiff feet need to flex. *Cushion shoes* promote flexibility and therefore promote neutral pronation.

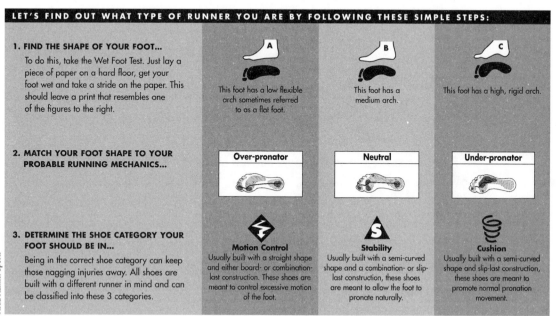

LET'S FIND OUT WHAT TYPE OF RUNNER YOU ARE BY FOLLOWING THESE SIMPLE STEPS:

1. FIND THE SHAPE OF YOUR FOOT...
To do this, take the Wet Foot Test. Just lay a piece of paper on a hard floor, get your foot wet and take a stride on the paper. This should leave a print that resembles one of the figures to the right.

A This foot has a low flexible arch sometimes referred to as a flat foot.

B This foot has a medium arch.

C This foot has a high, rigid arch.

2. MATCH YOUR FOOT SHAPE TO YOUR PROBABLE RUNNING MECHANICS...

Over-pronator

Neutral

Under-pronator

3. DETERMINE THE SHOE CATEGORY YOUR FOOT SHOULD BE IN...
Being in the correct shoe category can keep those nagging injuries away. All shoes are built with a different runner in mind and can be classified into these 3 categories.

Motion Control
Usually built with a straight shape and either board- or combination-last construction. These shoes are meant to control excessive motion of the foot.

Stability
Usually built with a semi-curved shape and a combination- or slip-last construction, these shoes are meant to allow the foot to pronate naturally.

Cushion
Usually built with a semi-curved shape and slip-last construction, these shoes are meant to promote normal pronation movement.

Road Runner Sports

The Right Shoe

Finally, you need to choose the right shoe within the category that best matches your foot characteristics.

Fit: The best shoe for you is the one that fits the best. This means that the heel and midfoot under your arch and across the laces are snug. The forefoot should be roomy to the point where you feel as if you could play the piano with your toes. Generally, one brand of shoes will fit your foot better than others. You'll probably have the best luck buying shoes within that brand.

Weight: The heavier you are, the more shoe you need under your foot. Generally, this means that you'll have to spend a few extra dollars to protect your foot.

Pace: Faster runners are more efficient runners. This means that they don't pound the pavement as much as slower runners and can wear lightweight running shoes.

Mileage: The more you run, the more shoe you need. Running injuries come from a number of things, but mostly they come from putting two and a half times your body weight on your shoe every time you take a stride. The more miles you run during a week, the more stress you put on your joints. Buying a more substantial shoe (that is, spending more money) will prevent nagging injuries. Also note that, like tires, most shoes are designed to be worn for a certain distance, then that's the end of their life. Be sure to ask how many miles the shoe you choose is designed for. Generally, the heavier the shoe, the more distance you can put on it.

Following these simple steps will put you in the right shoe for your running. Wearing the right shoes will let you run more often with less chance of injury.

Ballet

Ballet class will help you develop muscle tone in your hips, arms, abdominals, and back. It will definitely help your posture. I took several ballet classes growing up but then forgot how wonderful it felt to be in class. Many dance studios offer adult classes, even for beginners. These classes give you a chance to learn balance, develop flexibility, and support your body. They may even give you an artistic flair.

Basic equipment: You, ballet shoes, tights, and shorts or leotards.

Location: Classrooms at dance schools and community centers.

Cost: Shoes, clothing, and instruction fees can range from $50 to $150.

How to start: Make a commitment to yourself, then find a class in your area. Check out the various studios for beginning adult ballet classes. See this as an opportunity to move and stretch out your body. Having a scheduled time and place that you've paid for can be good motivation to follow through and not miss any classes.

Bicycling

Bicycling is one way to burn lots of calories, and it's a non-weight-bearing exercise. Since bicycling really works your lower body, it helps build and tone your leg muscles. And you can ride frequently, since it is not as jarring on the bones and joints as running. Start riding to that errand rather than driving. Make sure to wear a helmet, and always ride with the traffic (on the right-hand side of the road), stopping at lights and stop signs. Cycling safety is key to your enjoyment.

Basic equipment: You, a road or mountain bike, a helmet, water, and sunscreen. If you're bicycling outdoors after dark, you also need reflective clothing, a flashlight, a buddy, and a cell phone.

Extra equipment to jazz up your workout: Clips or clipless pedals; specialized components on the bike; a better, lighter, stronger bicycle; gloves; and cycling clothing.

Location: Roads or trails, or even indoors with a turbotrainer, which lets you ride your bicycle on rollers, staying in one place. (Or you can just get a stationary bike or use one at a health club.) When riding in traffic, follow

It's a bike!

the regular rules for auto traffic, but be aware that you're invisible to most drivers. Play it safe and keep alert.

Cost: You can borrow or buy used equipment or spring for new. Depending on what you get, you can pay anywhere from $150 to $4,000.

How to start: Make a commitment to yourself. Remember the fun you had as a kid rolling down the road? Now you can move farther and faster, while getting a good workout. Make biking an adventure and an opportunity to explore new areas. Tackle the trails (learn how to fall off safely) or just run errands.

Bicycle Tips for Beginners

I asked John Howard for some suggestions to help out beginner bicyclists. John is a three-time Olympic cyclist, Pan Am Games gold medalist, fourteen-time United States Cycling Federation and National Off Road Biking Association national champion, Ironman winner, former world speed record holder (at 152 mph), author of four cycling books, U.S. Bicycling Hall of Famer, and director of the International Cycling School of Champions, which gives week-long training sessions all over the country. For more information, you can contact him at johnduke@multisports.com.

1. Make sure you are correctly positioned on your bike. Good bike positioning will not only allow greater muscular force, but it will also make you more comfortable so that you can sustain your momentum.

2. Set the saddle. As a rule, you will want your saddle adjusted for about thirty-five to forty degrees of leg extension at the bottom of the stroke. This saddle position will give you more power, comfort, and safety.

3. Find the right saddle tilt. Of all the different factors that can alter your "feel" for riding, saddle tilt is very important. Set the nose too high, and it will feel like a split cinder block. Set it too low, and you will find yourself slipping forward, overtaxing the muscles in your thighs. Instead, try a neutral position, adjusting it with a carpenter's level, with the bike sitting on a flat floor.

4. Get comfortable with your pedals. Perhaps the most embarrassing and potentially dangerous situation for a cyclist is not being able to "clip out" of his or her pedal system at a traffic stop. For this reason, I recommend that before you even see the street, you spend some time perfecting your "twisted ankle" technique of rapid exit and entry. A good place to do this is on a spin-bike. You also may borrow or buy a stationary bicycle trainer to ensure successful duplication of this critical technique.

5. Go aero. Even a beginner can simulate an aerodynamic profile by using low, flat aerodynamic handlebars. Remember, wind slows you down more than anything else, so even small improvements in body streamlining, such as flattening the back and bending the elbows, will pay big dividends in terms of performance.

6. Loosen up. Although cycling is a power sport, a greater range of motion—especially in the hip area—will give you better access to the bigger muscle groups. I enjoy my ride a lot more when I spend fifteen minutes stretching before going out. In fact, I prefer to spend that much time stretching even if it means I have less time to ride.

7. Get stronger. Speed and power are second cousins, so strengthening all the major muscle groups involved in the motor action of pedaling will help a lot when you actually apply your strength to the road. To build up those muscles, work out in the gym.

8. Wear a helmet. There is absolutely no excuse for not wearing a bike helmet every time you hit the road. Your head is very delicate (and an amazingly useful addition to your anatomy), so demonstrate your intelligence by protecting it.

9. Know how to change a tire. It sounds silly, but a lot of us who think we can change a tire may miss a few critical steps along the way. Find a good shop that teaches this technique, learn it right, and then practice until you can do it properly.

10. Go to school. You might think riding a bike is a no-brainer, since you probably learned the skill when you were five or so years old. Think again. Cycling can be a complicated sport. For those who want to make this their sport, I recommend picking a good camp, learning proper riding skills from a professional, and having some fun in the process.

Success Story: Renee

When Renee turned fifty, she was at an all-time high of 250 pounds and knew it was time to change her life and get healthy. For years she had dieted off and on, but she could never seem to get it together. "I was determined this time to not only lose the weight but to keep it off," she says.

Renee has lost forty-six pounds so far and has gone from a size 24W to a size 18W. But this time she is focusing not just on her diet but also on a new commitment to developing a healthy lifestyle. She has started following the right path to a future that is filled with confidence and offers a brighter health outlook.

"I thought I would stop by now," she says. "But I feel so good about myself and my body that I can't stop. I never thought my life could be so wonderful now that I have started to make some healthy changes."

Renee gets up at 6:00 A.M. during the week to walk. On the weekend, she pops in her new best friend Denise Austin's workout video. She also participates in her company's aerobics class after work once a week and hopes to build up to more times a week.

She has participated in a few road races as well, including a 10K event to benefit the March of Dimes, a 5K race, and a 5K walk to raise funds to battle heart disease. In anticipation of a 10K walk to benefit the United Negro College Fund, she wrote to all her previous sponsors and said, "If you donate one dollar over last year's pledge, I will do the 10K course twice!" One person actually pledged a thousand dollars, and Renee did walk the course twice.

"I have never felt this good about myself," she says. "It keeps me going. I even find that I walk with more confidence now."

Renee started by making small changes that have had a big impact. She doesn't eat fried foods anymore and eats brown rice instead of white. Her bread is light or no-fat wheat. And she has gone from drinking whole milk to drinking 1 percent milk.

"Now my eating routine includes bringing a lunch to the office every other day and going to the company cafeteria on the alternate days," she notes. "I know how to make healthy food choices. I have even established Saturday as treat night, when I have something I enjoy without guilt.

"I think a test of my commitment to a healthier lifestyle of eating and exercising came when I worked at the state fair during my vacation. I continued my daily walking routine, brought my lunch to the fair, and stayed away from the areas with fatty foods. I knew that if I could make it through fair week, I could get through anything."

Moral support has been key to Renee's success, as she has received help from her coworkers, family, and friends. "At the fair, people knew I was trying to stay away from those foods. So if someone came by with them, they made sure to say, 'Renee doesn't eat that way anymore.' I still have my treat night, so during the fair I'd have a slice of pizza or a hot dog on Saturday. But I now practice moderation."

Renee is no longer self-conscious about her body or her weight. "I'm even wearing a little-heel shoe now. I was walking into the office the other day and caught a reflection of myself, and I thought, 'Hey, I'm getting a little bit of a shape.'

"My life has never been more filled with confidence. This is all because I made a commitment to get healthy. I even eat steamed veggies now, something I never did before. My tastes have changed, and so has my outlook on me and my life."

Cross-Country Skiing

Talk about an awesome cardio workout! When winter sets in and outdoor activities are limited, cross-country skiing can get you outside and give you a full-body workout. Moving your legs and arms in rhythm does take some getting used to, but with practice and instruction, you can glide across the snow with ease.

Basic equipment: You, ski boots and poles, cross-country skis, warm clothing, a helmet, and gloves.

Extra equipment to jazz up your workout: More technical and/or lightweight skis.

Location: Snow-covered trails and country runs at parks and resorts.

Cost: Cross-country skiing isn't nearly as expensive as downhill skiing. A complete outfit (poles, boots, skis, and bindings) can run you $300 to $400. It's best to rent everything until you're sure you enjoy the sport, and you can usually buy good used equipment in the fall at ski shops and sporting goods stores. Trail fees also are much cheaper than lift tickets, typically anywhere from $4 to $15 a day. Cross-country skiing requires minimal instruction, and you can usually find inexpensive group lessons at any ski resort or through your local ski shop.

How to start: Make a commitment to yourself. Then all you need is snow and a ski rental shop—and maybe a lesson or two. You can cross-country ski without any instruction, but it's nice to know how to stop, how to go uphill, and how to turn. (Those things do come in handy!)

Golf

Maybe golf doesn't burn a lot of calories, but you can get in some exercise by walking the course instead of renting a cart. Carrying your golf bag will help strengthen your upper body. In California, some golfers actually run from tee to tee in what they call Xtreme Golf. For the rest of us, golf is just a good way to get outside, walk a bit, and enjoy some nice weather and friends.

Basic equipment: You, golf clubs, a hat, and sunscreen.

Extra equipment to jazz up your workout: More or better clubs and golf shoes.

Location: Public and private courses, pitch-and-putts, and driving ranges.

Cost: You have to schedule a tee time (don't be late) and pay a greens fee that can be anywhere from $15 to hundreds of dollars, depending on the course. Private courses also charge a membership fee; some charge extra fees for country club benefits.

How to start: Make a commitment to yourself. Golf is a nice outdoor social sport. Although it's not the most aerobic activity, the walk will do you good, the swinging motion will help tone those love handles, and lugging your golf clubs around will substitute for a strength-training workout.

Running

I know from experience that running burns some serious calories, and it will definitely improve your overall fitness level and endurance. The key is to build up your running distance no more than 10 percent a week. Before you can run, you must walk. I started slowly with running (see page 115). I built up to running by alternating between intervals of walking and run-

It's always nice to have a crowd cheer you on.

ning. Each week I added a little more running to the routine. It took me seventeen minutes to complete my first mile, but it was the best mile I had ever run—best because I was *running* the whole time. Most people make the mistake of trying to run too much too soon, risking burnout and injury.

Basic equipment: You, running shoes, a hat, water, and sunscreen. If you're running outdoors after dark, you also need reflective clothing, a flashlight, a buddy, and a cell phone. (See "Finding the Shoe That Fits" on page 48.)

Extra equipment to jazz up your workout: A digital step counter, a heart rate monitor, special training and racing shoes, and technical running clothes.

Location: Outside on an outdoor track, along trails, or in your neighborhood. Inside on a treadmill or indoor track.

Cost: Minimal. The key is to invest in good-quality running shoes; expect to pay $60 to $140. For running indoors, you'll need a health club membership or a good-quality treadmill ($900 to $2,000).

How to start: Make a commitment to yourself. Remember that each day you run, you will feel better. Schedule your time to run just like any other appointment. Make sure to lay out your shoes and clothing so you don't forget and you can get going quickly. Remember to warm up before you run and cool down afterward. If you're running outside, enjoy your surroundings and take the opportunity to explore. If you're running on a treadmill, appreciate the time alone.

Swimming

Swimming is an excellent exercise that involves no pounding on the body's joints and muscles. Plus, when you sweat, you are already in the water, so it isn't as noticeable. Swimming really works your upper and lower body. And if you have problems with your knees or back, are recovering from an injury, are pregnant, or are older, swimming might be a good choice for you. My aunt Marge is sixty-three years old and has been swimming competitively since she was a kid. She now competes successfully at the Senior Games and proves every day that swimming is for everyone.

My early memories of swimming are from the YMCA in South Bend, Indiana. I was in swimming classes for kids, where you move up from minnow to shark. I didn't get much past minnow. Swimming never was a major part of my life, and as I gained weight, it was tougher and tougher to even consider putting on a swimsuit, let alone go to the pool. Find the strength to go to the pool and swim some laps. It will help your body without the impact, and the water can be quite refreshing.

I am amazed at the number of new people I met when I joined a masters swim class. I always thought I would join when I got better at swimming, but then I realized that you get better by joining. In any exercise group, there are different levels of skill and talent. A masters swim class is just an adult swim class. You don't have to be a master; you just have to be over eighteen. Don't be intimidated to be part of one.

Many of the people I met in that class were the same ones I saw at running races. I remember doing a 5K race and seeing a group of people standing around talking while I was off by myself. I saw them again on the course. Race after race, I watched them. More than a year later, when I joined the masters swim class, I finally met some of the people from that group—Kelly Krieger, Kara Kays, and Dave Brown—and they have become friends. Each of them, in their own way, have had a huge influence on me. Their spirit, talent, and kindness in helping me reach my goal of participating in triathlons have been wonderful. And just think, I lost a year of their friendship because I was afraid to take a swim class.

Basic equipment: You, a swimsuit, a swim cap, and goggles.

Extra equipment to jazz up your workout: Pool toys such as paddles, fins, and a kickboard; a swim stroke monitor; a lap counter; and a wet suit.

Location: Indoor or outdoor pool at your health club, community center, YMCA or YWCA, or masters swim club. Even the neighbor's outdoor pool can provide an opportunity for you to get in some laps. If the weather permits, open-water swimming in a lake or ocean can be an exhilarating alternative. People swim in San Francisco Bay all year round, even with water temperatures as low as fifty-three degrees.

Cost: You will have to pay a fee to swim anywhere but your own or your neighbor's pool. Masters swim clubs charge a fee that covers both coaching and use of the pool. Expect to pay $65 to $150 monthly, depending on your area. Some health clubs offer swim-only memberships for a lower fee.

How to start: Make a commitment to yourself. Believe it or not, water is a great equalizer when it comes to exercise. Schedule your time to swim just like any other appointment. Find a way to get over the "swimsuit issue" (see below), and you can have a great workout without stressing your joints or sweating. Consider taking a water aerobics class. These classes cater to larger, older, and injured people.

The Swimsuit Issue

I know that if you are overweight, one of the last things you want to do is get into a swimsuit and go out in public. Trust me; I feel it, too. It's always intimidating to expose so much of my body for others to see.

But swimming is one of the great equalizers for all body shapes. It doesn't put any stress on the joints, it's relaxing and refreshing because of being in the water, it stretches out the body, and it's appropriate for all fitness levels. I could go on and on about the great benefits of swimming, but for many of you, it will still come down to having to wear a swimsuit in public.

Well, you're just going to have to stop being so vain and remember why you are going to the pool. Focus on the feeling you will get from the exercise. Think about how you are improving your health. And develop a few strategies for the pool, such as finding out when it is the least crowded. Go then, and fewer people will see you. And in reality, the people who are there will be too busy working out to look at you anyway.

Shop for a new-style swimsuit that will cover more of your body. I always wore a black one-piece suit because everyone says black makes you

Nothing like an early morning swim.

Lauri Levenfeld, Zoom Photography, California

look slimmer. Now I wear a one-piece suit with a shorts-style bottom. One of my friends puts on a cover-up and sits at the edge of the pool, removing the cover-up just before she slips into the water to swim laps. Once she's in the water, her weight isn't an issue anymore—and not just because she's hidden from view.

I remember a woman who came to the pool on Saturdays during lap hours. She probably weighed more than four hundred pounds. But each Saturday she came at the same time, walked to her lane, got in, and swam up and back for hours. She always swam those laps in a sidestroke style and seemed to have such peace and joy about her. She also had a lot of grace in the water. My masters coach once said that she was one of the most consistent lap swimmers there.

Don't let your weight get in the way of your enjoying a wonderful exercise such as swimming. Walk in with your head held high. Most people will recognize that you are there to do something for your body and your health. But first *you* must recognize that you are doing something good for yourself.

Success Story: Kristi

Kristi is only twenty-five years old, but she got caught in the career trap as a software engineer and spent her entire day thinking and worrying about her job. She didn't feel as though she had the time to go to the gym and work out. For lunch she ate junk food from the vending machine or grabbed a quick burger or pizza. She was gaining weight, but, being young, she felt that she could lose it anytime she wanted.

"I felt like I was cheating my company if I went to the gym during lunch," she says. "I decided that if I was going to get to the top, I would have to be dedicated—twenty-four hours a day, seven days a week."

Each day was scheduled from the minute she woke up until the time she went to bed. Meeting after meeting after meeting. Planning sessions. Classes in new technology. The one thing she didn't leave time for was herself.

"We had a formal office Christmas party coming up," she says. "I pulled a dress out of the closet and couldn't even zip it up. That's when I realized that I needed to schedule myself into my daily planner."

Because she had swum in high school, she looked for a pool and a masters swim program in her neighborhood. "With the weight I was carrying, I wasn't looking forward to putting on a swimsuit," she says with a laugh. "But I found a program at an indoor pool so I could swim all year round."

The fact that the program was at 6:00 A.M. actually was a positive for her. "I didn't figure there would be huge crowds of people there that early to see what I looked like in a Speedo."

Besides the great feeling of working out, Kristi also found a side benefit that she hadn't thought about. "While I was swimming, I was solving work-related problems. You have a lot of time to think when you're in the water, and I'd finish those workouts invigorated for the day and with solutions to problems that I had been working on for weeks. Swimming was perfect for me. Having someone on the pool deck to tell me what to do was great; it eliminated any thinking at all. Now, whenever I travel on business, I make sure either the hotel has a pool or there is a pool or masters program in the area. I find that the pool is where I do my best thinking. That's my quiet time. I get out every time feeling like I have cleansed every pore in my body. I'm refreshed, pumped up, and ready for the day."

Of course, just adding swimming to her daily planner wasn't enough. Kristi also had to take a hard look at the food she was putting into her body.

"It's funny, when you're just sitting at your desk, it seems okay to eat pizza and burgers every day," she says. "But when I started swimming, somehow I didn't want to ruin the high from the workout with fatty foods. I started to eat more vegetables and fruits. In fact, I would go to the grocery store on my way to work after my swim and pick up fruit for the week. That's what I would snack on at my desk."

The other positive by-product for Kristi? By swimming from 6:00 to 7:00 A.M., she is usually able to get to her desk before 8:00 A.M. She misses the heavy traffic that she used to have to deal with at 8:30, plus she has a good half hour on the rest of her office mates.

"Being in an empty office allows me the quiet time I like to have at the beginning of the day," she says. "It's funny. All I wanted to do was add a little fitness to my life and get back into my old clothes. Swimming has made me better at my job and helped me feel better about myself."

Tennis

Okay, so I can't say I am even a remotely good tennis player. When I was a teenager, my friend Amanda and I played often. But after a while, I would start goofing around, trying to hit the ball over the high fences. In all seriousness, though, tennis is a sport that can really get you moving. It can improve the flexibility in your hips and shoulders and help tone your legs, calves, arms, shoulders, and upper back. Tennis courts are available both indoors and outdoors for year-round play.

Basic equipment: You, a tennis racket, court shoes, and a partner.

Extra equipment to jazz up your workout: Tennis clothing, a better racket, and lessons.

Location: Many health clubs offer indoor and/or outdoor courts. Look for tennis-only clubs, or check out local schools for outdoor courts you can use for free.

Cost: Depending on court fees, lessons, and the equipment you choose, costs can run $50 to $200.

How to start: Make a commitment to yourself. Then make a date to play tennis with someone. You will have the motivation of having another person depending on you to be there to return the serve. Enjoy the game!

Strength Training

Whatever else you do to cross-train, you should be doing some strength training twice a week. You are not going to get big or bulky by lifting weights unless you plan to spend hours in the weight room. We women just don't have the hormones to get muscle-bound. You will find a great number of benefits to adding strength training to your cardio routine. It can help strengthen your bones and thus lower your risk for osteoporosis. Think about your future and minimize those potential fractures by making your body stronger.

Here is another incentive to start hitting those weights and lifting those dumbbells: muscle burns more calories than fat. So if you can turn fat into muscle, you will boost your metabolism. And, yes, muscle does weigh more than fat, so sometimes the scale will be deceiving. That is why the tape measure, body fat testing, or the fit of your clothing can be a better indicator of your progress than the scale.

Visit your local health club and get instructions for using the machines. Have a trainer set up a program to help you reach your health goals by adding strength training to your routine.

Basic equipment: You, free weights, weight-lifting equipment, and lifting gloves.

Extra equipment to jazz up your workout: A personal trainer and instructional videos.

Location: All health clubs offer some type of strength-training equipment, from machines to dumbbells. Many people work out very effectively at home with basic dumbbells or resistance bands.

Cost: A health club membership can cost anywhere from $150 to $2,000 annually, but that includes some supervision and all the strength-training equipment you'll need. Personal trainers charge $25 an hour and up. Videos and books offering routines for dumbbells and resistance bands range from $5.95 to $49.95, but some TV programs offer workouts for free. You can spend anywhere from $45 to thousands of dollars for home gym equipment.

How to start: Make a commitment to yourself. This activity can do more for your overall toning, shaping, and slimming than anything else you do. You can lift weights anywhere—at a health club, at home, at a sports show, or in a hotel room. Work out with a trainer or a buddy to begin with. You'll need someone to spot you and make sure you're doing the lifts correctly. Incorporate strength training into your schedule twice a week, and you'll see benefits almost immediately.

Yoga

Yoga provides a good balance to cross-training. For thousands of years, yoga has helped people bridge the mental and physical parts of their being. I find it very relaxing—not to mention how great my body feels afterward. Yoga is for everyone, no matter what your fitness level. It's great for centering your breathing, thinking, and energy, and it can help start your day off right or take the stress out of a long day. Yoga involves a lot of stretching, and some types of yoga can be very aerobic. You will need an instructor at first to teach you the proper positions and techniques. Look for classes in your area to start learning the basics. This is a great opportunity to take a new look at your fitness routine and add a new exercise to your day.

Basic equipment: You, a mat, and loose-fitting clothing.

Extra equipment to jazz up your workout: Classes, videos, and music.

Location: Yoga is taught in workshops, private classes, health clubs, and community centers. Once you learn the basics, you can keep taking classes or invest in a book or video and do yoga at home.

Cost: Class fees range from $50 to $150 per course.

How to start: Make a commitment to yourself. Becoming part of a class will help keep you motivated. You also will learn about your body and how it moves. Yoga is a great stress reducer and is very relaxing. And you'll meet a new network of friends through yoga classes.

CHAPTER 5

Don't Go It Alone

The way a team plays as a whole determines its success. You may have the greatest bunch of individual stars in the world, but if they don't play together, the club won't be worth a dime.

—BABE RUTH

It's not always easy to find a group to work out with, but exercising in a group or with a friend can be the best way to stay motivated. You might not feel like going out for a walk one day, but if you're supposed to meet a friend to walk with, you'll make the effort.

Having a workout buddy makes exercise more fun for most people. You can talk while you walk, run, or even bicycle side by side. It's one way to make sure you're not working too hard. It also makes exercise a social outing instead of just work.

Working out with a friend or a group forces you to set a regular time to exercise. If you work out at the same time for a few weeks, you get into a workout habit. You stop thinking about whether or not to go. You just think, "It's time to get ready and go work out." You don't forget and make an appointment or plan to be somewhere else during your workout time. It becomes part of your regular weekly schedule, like going to church, picking up your kids from school, or watching your favorite TV show.

Exercise will be part of your life. And surprisingly, you'll find that even if your workout buddy bails out on you or your group falls apart, you'll want to keep going.

I remember one time I was all ready to play volleyball for the evening. I waited and waited, only to find out that most of the team had called in to

It's good to have support—I couldn't do this without my friends. Lauri Levenfeld, Zoom Photography, California

say they were not going to be able to make it that evening. I understood because most of the players in the pickup league were busy professionals. I was disappointed, though, because I had come to depend on those games. But instead of going home, I headed to the fitness area to work on the cardio machines. In some ways, it was a good opportunity for me to break out and start doing some exercise on my own. My goal was not just to play volleyball at a set time each week but to get moving more. Volleyball gave me the motivation to show up at the health club, but I now found that I had the motivation to be there no matter what.

Get Fitter Faster

Teaming up with a friend can help you get fitter faster. Try to find someone at about the same fitness level to exercise with. Someone who's much fitter can coach you and help you along, but not everyone is a good coach. A fitter friend might set a pace you can't keep up with, and you'll end up feeling frustrated and quit. Someone who's a lot more out of shape than you isn't a good choice either. That will just give you an excuse to slow down.

Working out with a friend who's at about the same fitness level allows you both to challenge and encourage each other and work together to set up a solid training schedule. Some people have several partners and trade off days—Tuesday with Marie, Thursday with Joan, and Saturday with their spouse, for instance.

It's not always easy to find someone who is at your fitness level and whom you like well enough to want to spend time with every week. Even worse, sometimes you'll find the perfect workout buddy, but that person will move, improve faster than you, or burn out and not want to exercise anymore. When that happens, you have to go back to square one and start looking for someone new. Don't let your partner drag you down.

It's often better to work out with a whole group. That way, one person's problems are less likely to affect you, and when one person misses a workout, it won't matter so much to you. Plus you can still enjoy all the social and fitness benefits.

Find Some Workout Partners

There are many ways to find potential workout partners.

1 **Advertise.** A lot of sporting goods stores have bulletin boards where you can post notices. Keep it simple: "Looking for someone to walk with on Mondays and Wednesdays. Beginner level, usually two miles. Call . . ."

2 **Check at your health club.** Some health clubs have bulletin boards, and most offer classes and group workouts. Although a personal friend is the most fun to work out with, there is a lot to be said for the motivation of paying for a class.

3 **Check at a bicycle shop.** These shops often have group rides. Just go in and ask the sales clerk about these and check out the bulletin board.

4 **Ask people at work.** You might be able to set up a before-work, lunchtime, or after-work fitness routine or join one that's already going.

5 **Ask at church or temple.** Again, use the bulletin board or church newsletter to let people know you're looking for workout partners. And talk to people. Tell them about your fitness goals and invite them to join you.

6 **Put up a notice at the grocery store or community center.** You might find out that a neighbor is interested.

7 **Check with your local parks and recreation department.** Many areas have ranger-led walks. These are usually instructional, so you won't be going too fast and you'll get a chance to learn about your area. It's not a bad way to start moving more, and you may meet people through these programs who are interested in having a workout partner or who already belong to an exercise group you can join.

8 **If you live in a college town, put up a notice on campus.** Don't be afraid to cast your net into a different environment. A wide variety of people live and work on campus—many of them health-conscious and interesting to talk with.

9 **If you can't find an existing group, start your own.**

10 **Have a virtual partner.** With so many people online these days, it's possible to have an online exercise buddy. You can check in with each other every day to confirm your progress.

Participate in Charity Events

One way to get involved in a group—often a big group—is to get involved in a charity. Nearly every running or walking race donates part of each entry fee to charity. Small events often have local beneficiaries, from schools to clubs, hospitals to arts festivals, individual help funds to civic programs. Larger events are often associated with major charities, such as the Red Cross, or with major causes, such as cancer research.

Choosing an event on the basis of the charity involved can be a real motivator. For example, the "pink ladies" at every Race for the Cure (to benefit breast cancer research) make a simple 5K into a moving and humbling experience. These women are breast cancer survivors, each living proof that medical research and physical fitness make a real difference in people's lives.

The Race for the Cure organization makes it easy for you to help. All you have to do is enter your local event—there are 5K runs/walks all over the country—and you contribute to local and national breast cancer research efforts and breast cancer initiatives. A 5K event is a reasonable goal for almost everyone, and you can feel part of something bigger than yourself as you train for it.

Following are some other wonderful organizations with fitness events.

Programs That Provide Training

Some charities ask you to raise a certain amount of money as part of the entry fee. They give you lots of support, including suggestions on how to raise money. Some even offer prizes as incentives. Some of the bigger charities offer you training to help you complete your race of choice.

The Arthritis Foundation is associated with races of various lengths across the country. It's best known for sending whole groups of runners to major marathons around the world to help raise funds for educational programs and research. The foundation provides round-trip airfare to the event, your entry fee, a place to stay, fund-raising support and materials, running clothes, and parties. It also provides a training program tailored to your fitness level, inspiration, a group of people with similar goals to work out with, and counseling on nutrition and injury prevention. Don't forget the fact that you get to feel good about yourself the whole time because you're not only running to get fit and becoming part of a wonderful group of people, but you're also helping others at the same time.

A Special Kind of Motivation

The Leukemia Society of America's Team in Training not only gives you training in exchange for fund-raising, but it also gives you a person to train for. The Honored Patient program pairs you with one or more leukemia patients.

You're not just running for research and education; you're also running for this person, whose name appears on a wristband that you wear during the race. Many people get to know their Honored Patient personally, and more than one has said that's what got them across the finish line. Others bring their own Honored Patient to the program—a friend or loved one who has been diagnosed with or has died from leukemia or lymphoma.

To join the Team in Training program, you must sign up for an event and a training program four to five months in advance. The society provides professional coaches and clinics on form, technique, equipment, injury prevention, race strategies, and nutrition. The coaching also enhances your strength, flexibility, endurance, and weight control. I have several friends who never thought they could run a marathon until they joined Team in Training. Still, you need to be reasonably fit before you start working toward a marathon. It helps a lot if you've already run or walked a 10K.

Individual fund-raising goals are high—an average of $3,200 for a marathon. For that you get race entry, transportation to the event, accommodations at the event, and both the training and motivation to get you across the finish line (not to mention tremendous fund-raising guidance and support). You'll see huge Team in Training groups at marathons all over the world. Take a good look. The members are a lot like you.

Programs That Focus on Women

Both the Race for the Cure and Avon Running Global Women's Circuit focus on women's running—Race for the Cure because it's fighting breast cancer, Avon Running because the company believes that women need support to attain health and fitness. Avon Running tries to provide practical exercise options for women. Its series of 10K runs, 5K walk/fun runs, and workshops gives you a

Getting a little help from a friend.

Lauri Levenfeld, Zoom Photography, California

71

realistic fitness goal and the opportunity to meet and develop friendships with other fitness-conscious women. One-third of your entry fee in an Avon Running event supports community running organizations.

Do It Yourself

Of course, you don't need to be part of a big organization to use your sport to help others. Some people put on their own sporting events to benefit a person or charity that is dear to their heart (some areas make this easier than others with looser permit requirements). Others simply approach business to sponsor them and their charities of choice. The idea is that you wear the logo of the business on your jersey, often paired with the charity name—CARING COMPUTERS SUPPORTS NEWARK BOYS CLUBS, for instance. The company gets some positive publicity, you get the motivation to compete and do your best, and the charity gets a donation.

Even easier, you can contribute to a charity simply by buying a good pair of shoes or running apparel. For example, Fila contributes part of every sale to the Ulman Cancer Fund for Young Adults. Probably the best way to find similar programs is on the World Wide Web. These programs may make it easier to choose between similar products from different manufacturers.

Look for information on charities that sponsor running programs in the Resources section of this book.

Success Story: Nancy

Nancy's story is very common. Always considered petite by her friends and family, Nancy gained forty pounds during the nine months that she carried Noah, her first child. After becoming a mom, no matter how hard she tried, she couldn't get rid of the twenty-five extra pounds that now seemed to be a permanent part of her life.

"I went to the gym and tried the same workouts I did before I was pregnant," she says. "I bought workout tapes that I could do at home, but nothing seemed to work."

Her problem was that her sleep patterns had changed. Sometimes Noah slept most of the night; sometimes he didn't sleep at all. When she was wide-awake at 2:00 A.M., Nancy would prop herself in front of the TV and eat Cheetos or whatever else she could find around the house.

"I wasn't eating because I was hungry," she admits. "I was eating because it was something to do."

For Nancy, finding out that two other women in the neighborhood were going through the same thing made all the difference. They had recently had children and couldn't get rid of their extra weight either. They recruited a few more friends and started their own workout group. Sometimes they used a Denise Austin workout tape to exercise together at one of the women's houses. They also went walking, taking turns baby-sitting. Nancy found that the social interaction was as important to her physical health as the workouts themselves. The women set goals as a group, deciding to do the Race for the Cure 5K six months after starting to work out together.

"When you work out as a group, you don't even feel that you are working out," Nancy says. "We spend social time together, and before we know it, we've walked three miles. Working out was never this easy before I had Noah."

Nancy also bought a Baby Jogger, an all-terrain stroller, so that she and Noah could go out for a nice brisk walk through the neighborhood by themselves or with one of the other moms. "Noah and I can go exploring anytime we want," she says. "The Baby Jogger provides this adventure time for us. When we go to Grandma's house, I fold up the Baby Jogger and bring it with me. There is no reason not to go out for a mile or two every day, no matter where we are. It's amazing. And Noah and I are both sleeping better, which I don't think is a coincidence."

Working out was something Nancy had always done to maintain her dress size. "Now it isn't just something I do, it's who I am. Every single day I am either working out at home with my friends, walking through the neighborhood with Noah, or exploring. In the past, I would never have gone for a walk by myself, but now I don't have to. There is strength, confidence, and security in numbers. I love the feeling that you get during a walk or right afterward. It's really special."

How to Start Your Own Workout Group

If you're a stay-at-home parent, it can be very hard to get out to exercise. One of the most flexible ways to deal with the problem is to start your own workout group and share responsibility for the kids. It's easier to do than you might think, and the children will benefit as well. The following steps work for a running, walking, or cycling group.

1 Advertise. Put up flyers at your local supermarket. Place an ad in your church or temple bulletin. Spend a couple of bucks and run an ad in the local newspaper. Just get the word out that you're starting an exercise group for parents.

2 Find a reliable baby-sitter. If you and your exercise buddies can't find someone you trust, take turns staying with the kids while the others run. Baby-sitters are not just for nights out on the town.

3 Find an appropriate place for child care. If the group becomes too big to keep all the kids at one house, contact a local recreation center or meeting hall to see if you can use or rent a room for one hour a couple of times a week.

4 Make sure someone in the group knows a little bit about your sport. Have the beginners start slowly and gradually increase their distance (no more than 10 percent a week). Don't be afraid to mix in some easier stuff. It's better to start slowly and make it last than to get injured, become frustrated, and quit.

5 Be safe. If some of the members haven't been exercising, make sure they get a physical and a doctor's okay. Beginners shouldn't exercise more than every other day.

6 Mix it up. Follow the hard-easy rule: a hard day followed by an easy day. Vary your location or course so that the workout stays fresh and fun.

7 **Stay out of traffic.** The point is to relax, not dodge tractor-trailers and inhale exhaust fumes.

8 **Set a goal.** Look for a local competition for which members of the group can train. A goal will give you the incentive to stick to the program.

The Racey Ladies

Jennifer Cunningham was suffering from postpartum depression. Here she was in her late twenties, a Cal Berkeley grad who had sacrificed her dietitian career to stay at home and raise her kids. And she felt as if she was going insane.

"I always thought I was this very mellow, easygoing, typical southern Californian," says Cunningham, who lives in Carlsbad, California, a beach city thirty miles north of San Diego. "But you have kids and you become this screaming, impatient maniac. I was *this* close to seeing a counselor."

Then she spotted an ad in a recreation center's bulletin. A group of women had hired baby-sitters at the rec center and were hitting the roads and trails by foot. Bye-bye, depression. Hello, running. Last March, Cunningham, after three years with her running group, ran her first marathon, covering the Napa Valley Marathon in three hours, fifty-eight minutes.

"I never thought I was the type of person who could run a marathon," says Cunningham, now thirty-two. "It was the ladies who encouraged me, saying, 'Of course you can.' It was an amazing feeling."

The group Cunningham tours San Diego's backcountry with is called the Racey Ladies. The founder, Sally Montrucchio, meets regularly with some of her old running partners. "This group gave us friendships that last a life-time," Montrucchio says.

Back in 1977, Montrucchio formed her own interior decorating business. She worked out of her home to be around her two young children. A competitive runner at the time, she kept bumping into women who wanted an exercise outlet but were confined to their homes with children. Montruc-

The Racey Ladies and their kids. Lois Schwartz

The Racey Ladies hit the trail. Lois Schwartz

chio hired a sitter and opened her home to the group, and the Racey Ladies were born.

At the time, few of them were budding Olympians. "A couple had maybe jogged in the past," Montrucchio says. "Most of them had never run in their lives."

"It took me three months before I could run three miles," says Bobbi Charmoli. Now fifty-one, she has completed seven marathons.

Montrucchio, who ran with her ex-husband, a former Olympic Trials marathoner, was both Racey Ladies founder and coach. She had the women start slowly—running some, walking some. She stressed body mechanics. She suggested the right shoes to buy. And she knows why the concept was a hit.

"Women love to talk," Montrucchio says. "If you're out there suffering and your mouth's flapping at the same time, you don't know you're suffering."

Starting primarily as a social outlet, the Racey Ladies evolved into some pretty dedicated runners. One day they were pelted by a howling rainstorm before being rescued by police officers.

"We ran a lot of times in the dark with flashlights," Charmoli says. "Somebody would carry a screwdriver. Animals were always out there. It was pretty stupid, but we couldn't miss a day."

As you'd expect, enduring friendships were formed. The group celebrated a child's birth and mourned a loved one's death. Montrucchio suffered through a divorce. Her running partners came to her support by baby-sitting. They cheered her up once by buying her a new dress. More important, they didn't desert her.

"They didn't walk away from me because I was divorced," Montrucchio says. "They gave my kids a sense of community.

"When you're pushing hard at something physically, it breaks down barriers mentally. You probably know more about each other than you should. There are no false pretenses."

Montrucchio's divorce forced her to work full-time selling real estate. She left the Racey Ladies after about seven years, but others have stepped in to fill the void. There have been as few as fifteen women consistently getting together and as many as thirty. Today the Racey Ladies meet three times a week.

Kit Brazier has run with the group longer than anyone else. Although her visits are less frequent now, maybe once a month, her membership goes back eighteen years. She says the Racey Ladies are more competitive now, although there are still some casual joggers and walkers. But the reasons behind the group's success are the same. "It's the camaraderie and something to keep you going," Brazier says.

Racey Lady Renee Richardson admits, "It brought the joy back to running. That's the best gift of all."

Her husband, Tony, says, "It sure beats Prozac."

Balancing her three-year-old son on her hip while shooing another little one to the family Suburban, Erin Antel said, "We're probably the happiest stay-at-home moms you'll ever find."

CHAPTER 6

Gyms Are Not Just for Bunnies, Models, and Pro Athletes

There is no failure until you fail to keep trying.
—ANONYMOUS

Steps for Finding a Health Club

Once you have a few sports in mind, you need to establish a place where you can do them. Finding a gym can be the first active step in starting and staying with your new goal of getting healthy by adding exercise to your life. No matter what size or shape you are, you can belong to a gym. Remember, fitness centers exist to help you get into shape. They are there for *you.*

There are a lot of reasons to join a gym and participate in exercise classes, but the most important one is that gyms employ people to instruct and support you in your goals. Whenever you have questions, someone is on hand to help. A gym is an environment where you can meet people who have similar goals, who may be looking for an exercise buddy, or who may need someone to play court sports with.

Finding the right gym, however, depends on many factors, including where you live; your budget, schedule, and need for child care; the classes you are looking for; and the availability of personal trainers, masseurs or masseuses, nutritionists, and other fitness specialists.

Health clubs are filled with equipment and classes designed to keep you moving. Some have pools for lap swimming, deep-water running, and water aerobics. If you are interested in court sports such as basketball, volleyball, tennis, and racquetball, they have facilities that allow you to play year-round.

So how do you go about finding the right health club? Here are a few questions to ask when looking for one.

1 **What is your budget?** Determine what you can afford to spend on a yearly membership before visiting the health clubs in your area. Health club membership fees can vary from $35 to $300 a month. No matter where you live, you can find a club to meet your needs and your budget. Often the more expensive clubs just have bigger bathrooms and plusher towels.

Check with your employer to see whether the company offers a reimbursement for joining a health club. Many clubs also offer periodic membership specials for joining, lower rates for longer contracts, or discounts on initiation fees. Get your membership contract in writing and review it before signing. Don't let the club pressure you with pushy sales tactics.

Some clubs have aerobics floors and a ton of equipment, but those things come with a price tag. Often clubs with swimming pools, indoor tracks, and sports courts cost more. Some clubs have locker room attendants and offer lots of pampering. By contrast, many YMCAs offer basic fitness programs that include strength training and swimming at a very low price.

The bottom line is, determine what you need out of a health club before you start shopping. Don't settle for less, but don't pay for more. For instance, if you are going to need to shower, look for things such as hair dryers and shampoo. But if you are going to go home to shower, you don't need a deluxe changing room. Find a place that you can afford, that has the equipment and programs you need, and that provides a comfortable atmosphere, then make a commitment to go there regularly.

2 **Is the club close to your work or home?** A major factor in making sure you go to the health club regularly is how accessible it is. After a long day at the office and a commute, it might be tough to go back out the door and drive twenty-five minutes to your health club. One option is to find a health club close to your office and make it part of your before- or after-work routine.

When I was living in Michigan, my health club was about a four-minute drive from my office. It was easy for me to do a morning workout and still get to work on time—with dry hair.

3 **Does the club have the type of facilities you want?** Once you set your goals, you should find out whether the health club has the classes and equipment to help you work toward those goals. If you want strength training, make sure the club has a good range of free weights, machines, dumbbells, mats, and mirrors. If you are looking for a cardio routine, check out the treadmills and other machines. If you want to swim, make sure the club has an indoor pool.

Since I do most of my running and cycling outside, I look for a club with a great lap pool and weights. I use the treadmills and stationary bikes on days when it's too cold to be outside.

A Side Note

The International Raquet Sports Health Association (IRSHA) is a governing organization for numerous health clubs across the country. If a health club you are visiting is part of that network, you can be assured good treatment and programs. Health clubs associated with IRSHA offer a passport program. Since I often traveled for work, I would look in the program booklet to see if there was an IRSHA club in the city I was visiting. I could use my home membership card to visit that club and pay just a small guest fee. With this program, I was able to work out in some of the best clubs in the country.

4 **Does it offer the type of activities you are interested in?** If you are interested only in tennis, look for a club that offers indoor and/or outdoor courts. If you enjoy dancing, look for a club with dance aerobics classes. Special classes in areas such as spin cycling, walking, rowing, yoga, kickboxing, wall climbing, circuit training, and health and wellness can add variety to your workout routine, but not every club offers them.

Before heading out to visit the health clubs, make sure you have a list of all the activities you are interested in now or think you might want in the future. Write them down so that you won't forget to ask about them. Take a look at the health club's class schedule to see what is available during the times you can be there.

5 **Is child care available?** Many clubs offer child care while you work out. That way, the kids get to play while you exercise, but you are nearby if anything happens.

6 **Is the club well maintained and clean?** This is the first thing I look for. You will be spending a considerable amount of time there, so make sure you are comfortable with the environment.

7 **Who uses the club during the times when you are most likely to be there?** Visit the club during the hours you are most likely to exercise. This is really important. It will help you determine what types of people you will face and how long you will have to wait to use the machines. Peak hours vary with each health club. Remember to ask about peak hours during your visit. Some clubs even charge more for peak hour usage. Early morning still seems to be the best time to go to a club.

8 **Do the club's hours correspond with your schedule?** Always grab a flyer that has the club's hours printed on it. That way, you can be sure that the club will be open when you are available. The schedule also will come in handy if you need to work out later or earlier than usual.

9 **Is the fitness staff certified?** If you are interested in personal training or fitness instruction, make sure that the trainers, fitness staff, and aerobics and other class instructors are certified. (See pages 86–87 to find out how to verify this.)

10 **Does the club offer a trial membership?** If you aren't sure about a health club after a tour of the facilities and meeting with the membership coordinator, ask about a free trial membership. Some clubs offer anywhere from a day to two weeks to try out the club. Or talk to your coworkers and friends to find out which health clubs they belong to and see if you can go as a guest. There is nothing like working out at a health club to get a sense of whether you will be comfortable there.

Judy's Gym Story

Joining a gym again can be a bit intimidating. The first time I joined a health club, I paid for the membership and never used it. Going to a health club—whether it's for the first or the seventh time—is a process.

The next time I joined a club, I went with a purpose: to get healthy. I was doing this for me, and I was not going to worry about what others were thinking. Of course, as I went on a tour of the gym, I wondered whether people were looking at me. But I focused on learning about the equipment they had and what kinds of services they provided. I just kept thinking, "This is for me. It doesn't matter what other people think." Once I joined, I was grateful that I had paid attention during the tour, because when I got there, I knew where the locker room was, where the classes were held, and so on.

In the beginning, no one talked to me. But once people started seeing me there regularly, they began to root me on.

Breaking into the locker room chitchat was a bit harder. Once I opened up and let them know what I was up to, people were a lot more receptive. They began to include me in their conversations and provide me with helpful information. One of the best bonding times I found was after the morning aerobics classes, when all of us would chat as we hurried to get ready for work. If you missed a day, everyone would ask where you were. It became like a support group.

I learned that it makes a difference if you go into a club with a positive attitude, are friendly, and are open to the experience. Everyone at the gym has his or her own struggle. For some, it may be a pound, for me, it was one hundred pounds. But the focus on staying healthy and the journey to fitness are similar for everyone.

CHAPTER 7

You Wouldn't Ask Your Dentist for Legal Advice

I just love when people say I can't do something because all my life people said I wasn't going to make it.

—TED TURNER

Find a Personal Trainer and a Coach

If you think that personal trainers are just for the rich and famous and that you could never afford one, it's not true. As with lawyers and doctors, sometimes you need them. Here are some considerations for how a personal trainer could help jump-start your routine, prevent injuries, and save you time and money in the long run.

When I first started to get fit again in 1994, I watched Oprah Winfrey. I saw her work with a personal trainer to help her reach her goals. I thought that if I had someone to push, teach, and motivate me, I could get into a fitness routine, too.

My first trainer, Jim, was awesome. He taught me how and why exercise is important. What he couldn't do was make me enjoy exercise, do the exercise for me, or help me deal with my eating issues.

I was floating aimlessly during that time. I had no real goals other than to lose a lot of weight. Jim was very honest with me. He explained that despite all the hours I was putting in, the weight was slow in coming off because of my nutrition.

Jim pointed out that he could help me get in shape but I needed help in getting my eating under control. I was working hard in the gym, and he encouraged me to reward myself with things like a manicure or a massage instead of fattening treats.

Then, in 1996, I broke my foot. I had just finished my first triathlon, and I went from being on top of the world to not being able to do any of my workouts. I finally asked my doctor if I could do strength training. He said, "Sure, but with crutches and a non-weight-bearing cast, it will be hard. You can't put any weight or force on that foot." This was when a trainer really became handy.

I was working in Columbus, Ohio, at the time, and working out at a health club. I wasn't using a personal trainer because Jim had taught me how to lift weights properly, emphasizing technique, so I was able to self-train. At this point, though, I needed help. I selected a trainer named Ben because I always saw him working at the club with women who had weight problems.

Ben had the experience to work around my injury and help me continue to get stronger despite the setback. People would tease him, saying, "Boy, you don't let anyone off the hook—even when they're wearing a cast!" It wasn't always fun, but Ben raised my spirits during a dark time.

It's a Trade-off

Remember that you are hiring a personal trainer for *you*. If at any time you aren't happy with your trainer, talk to him or her about your concerns. I once had a personal trainer who wasn't working out. I explained all my goals, but he continued to set up exercises as if I wanted to look like Arnold Schwarzenegger. I wanted to train for triathlons, not bodybuild. So I finally said, "No more." I lost some money, but I learned a valuable lesson: value your goals and not someone else's.

Personal trainers can be an important component of your fitness program, providing experience and support that will help you reach all your health and fitness goals. Yes, a trainer is an investment, but think of it as an investment in your health and wellness. Sometimes you have to make choices. To afford a trainer, I drive an old car. I choose health over a lot of other things.

Here are a few things you can try to ease the financial burden.

1 **Find a friend** and see if the trainer will train both of you at the same time. That way, you can split the training fee.

2 **Consider buying a set training package** and have the personal trainer instruct you in how to lift weights properly and safely for a few sessions. Then have the trainer design a program that you can follow on your own for several weeks. At that point, you might need only one session with the trainer every week or two to check on your progress and update your program.

3 **Check with your health club** to see if it offers programs for circuit training with weights. The health club I belonged to in St. Joseph had a creative fitness director named Michelle who would set up classes in which people could lift various weights in a circuit. For such a class, you pay a small fee to have an experienced trainer supervising the class, you get a great strength-training workout, and you don't have the expense of training solo.

4 **Take a class.** Pay attention to local health clubs' bulletin boards and newsletters for classes on how to lift weights. Some clubs set up programs for "women on weights" to help get you started properly.

Make an Educated Choice

Here are some tips to help you find a personal trainer who's right for you and your goals.

1 **Trainer's certification.** The first step in making sure a trainer is qualified is to verify that he or she is certified through a national organization. Look for certification by an organization such as the American College of Sports Medicine

(ACSM), the National Strength and Conditioning Association (NSCA), the American Council on Exercise (ACE), or the Aerobics and Fitness Association of America (AFAA). Certification assures you that a prospective trainer is educated in health and fitness and that he or she is up on the latest issues. Many personal trainers have additional college training or a degree in exercise-related fields. All personal trainers are required to be certified in cardiopulmonary resuscitation (CPR) and first aid.

Don't be afraid to ask to see the trainer's certificate(s). If the trainer is in a health club environment, the club should have these records on file.

2 **Trainer's experience.** Remember, you're the customer here. It's important to discuss the personal trainer's background. How long has he been a personal trainer? How many people has he trained? What are most of his client's goals? Does he have expertise in working with overweight people, runners, and people with injuries—people like you? Ask the trainer for references from people he has trained, and talk to his clients to give you an idea of what he is like. Watch the trainer working with others to see his behavior, style, and attitude. A good personal trainer will not take offense; it's part of his business to supply the information you need to choose wisely.

3 **Trainer's philosophy.** Make sure that you talk to the trainer about her workout philosophy and that it matches your goals. There is a big difference between bodybuilding and toning those thighs.

4 **Trainer's availability.** Check out the trainer's schedule. Make sure he has time available based on your schedule. Some trainers are very busy and popular. If you need a certain time slot, make sure it is available. Also ask about the trainer's cancellation policy.

5 **Trainer as mentor and role model.** Find a personal trainer who can motivate and inspire you. You don't want someone who will just pull and place the pins. It helps, too, if she can teach you the whys as well as the hows—why you are doing a certain machine, how the muscle works, and so on. If you don't care about those things, tell the trainer that so that you can both avoid some aggravation. In addition, a personal trainer should be a role model and should practice what she preaches.

6 Your budget. Your budget will play a big part in hiring a trainer. Personal training sessions can range from $25 to $150 per hour, depending on the city and the club. Know what you can afford and stick to your budget. Keep looking until you find a trainer and a program that work for you financially as well as physically. Don't let money be an excuse to drop out of a program. Shop around at various health clubs and studios and among various trainers who meet your budget. If you find a trainer whom you like but who is too expensive, talk to him. He might know someone you can partner up with, he might be willing to discount his rate if you can work out at odd hours, he might have a class you would fit into, or he might know another trainer who charges less. Find out your options.

7 Your goals. You need to provide the trainer with some information about yourself. Be clear on your goals. Make sure they match up with the trainer's experience. Also make sure the trainer has a system for fitness assessment and health screening—and a checklist for any medical problems you might have. The trainer also should have a system to track your progress toward specific goals. This can mean regular fitness assessments and body fat testing to mark your progress.

Although you need to be open to your trainer's advice, you should both agree on workout goals based on a preliminary health screening and fitness assessment. These goals should be realistic and attainable.

8 Personality. Personality plays an important role here. You are planning to spend time with this person one-on-one, so you want to make sure you get along and can communicate. Some people do best when they're pushed hard; others do best with a gentler kind of support. Think about the kind of person you are and the kind of "boss" you respond well to. Look for someone you will want to please and someone you won't resent, because the trainer's job is to make you work. This is the *personal* part of *personal trainer,* and it can be the difference between great results and dropping out.

9 **Insurance coverage.** Check with your health club to make sure it has insurance that will cover you if you are injured due to your trainer's negligence. Insurance coverage is especially important if you have a personal trainer come to your home or if you go to the trainer's studio.

Get a Coach

After a while, I was comfortable working with a personal trainer, but trainers mostly work in the gym, focusing on strength training, cardiovascular fitness, and, sometimes, nutrition and nutritional supplements. For help in training for a particular sport—running, swimming, cycling, multisports, or team sports—you need a coach. I was lucky enough to find a coach who was able to help me develop an exercise plan that would keep me headed toward my goal of completing a triathlon.

Look for a coach whose expertise can help you reach your personal goals, whatever they might be. Coached workouts can keep you from getting hurt, can help you stay motivated, and can provide at least one organized workout every week where someone is checking your progress and making sure you're doing things right.

You don't have to have face-to-face contact with your coach, although that's probably best. More and more coaches are communicating with athletes via phone, fax, and E-mail. My coach was in Maryland and I was in Michigan, and we worked very well together.

Coach Troy

In April 1996, when I decided to do an Olympic-distance triathlon event, I already had several 5K races under my belt. But when it came to the triathlon, I knew I needed a lot of assistance. I started by asking the fitness staff and personal trainers at the health club I belonged to. Did they know how to train for a

Me with Coach Troy.

triathlon? Could I do one? They were all very supportive, but they didn't have any experience in that particular event. One of them suggested that I contact the sport's governing organization.

By looking on the Internet, I found the Triathlon Federation, now called USA Triathlon. I called the number provided, and a recording recommended a coach the organization had on staff. When I spoke to him, I explained that I lived in a small town that didn't have any triathlon groups or coaches. He asked me what larger cities I lived near, and I said Chicago, Ann Arbor, Lansing, and Kalamazoo. He knew of triathlon groups in Chicago and Ann Arbor, but he was not aware of any coaches in those areas. He suggested that I contact the local organizations to find out whether they had any coaches.

Shortly thereafter, I was at a sporting goods store, looking through the magazine rack. I was already reading *Runner's World,* which helped me with running advice and information. Now I picked up an issue of *Triathlete.* I purchased it and read every page. At the back of the magazine, in the classified ads under the heading "Training," there was an ad for triathlon coaching by Troy Jacobson, a sub-nine-hour Ironman competitor.

The ad read, "Coach Troy Jacobson, Personal Training Systems for Your Personal Best!" It went on to say, "Let me develop a custom training plan to fit YOUR busy schedule. I can help you achieve your goals regardless of your time, ability, or experience."

I called right away and left a message to let him know I was interested in his coaching services. That was in May 1996. When he returned my phone call a few days later, I told him, "I am very overweight. I don't know anything about triathlons. I don't own a bike or a swimsuit. But I want to lose some weight and finish this triathlon race in August happy and smiling."

That was my goal—to finish the race happy and smiling. We talked for quite a while. I told Troy, "I have the desire and the dedication to do this. I just need to be helped in how much to do and when."

We spoke for more than an hour about my goals, current fitness level, and expectations. It felt right. He told me he used to be a football player weighing more than 235 pounds. Through the triathlon, he had reshaped his life and himself into a 175-pound top professional athlete. He even told me about a woman he trained with who was the same height as I am, five-foot-eleven. From this, I saw that he knew what I was struggling with and that I could do this sport no matter what my weight or height.

My First Training Program

After we spoke again, I told Troy I was ready to start training with him. A few weeks later, I received my first training program. I was so thrilled to start a new program. I felt I was really going to reach my goals. I still have that first program as a reminder of where I started—you can see a facsimile of it on the next page.

Shortly after Troy received my fitness questionnaire and medical evaluations, he told me, "This year, in 1996, you will finish the triathlon you're aiming for. Next year, you will do ten to twelve, and then you will do an Ironman."

I remember laughing and saying, "I'm just going to do one and lose some weight and get healthy. That's it. And no way will I ever do an Ironman—I'm too big!"

But Troy was right. I completed my first Olympic-distance triathlon on August 10, 1996, and in 1997 I went on to complete eight triathlon races (including two Half Ironman distance events). I would probably have done more that year, but I did several road races, too. In 1998, I attempted the Hawaii Ironman.

•

Having supportive people around you to serve as cheerleaders is great. But it is also important to find fitness professionals, trainers, and coaches who can give you

Date: 6/13–6/20

Goals:

Day	Swim	Bike	Run
Mon	off	off	off
Tues	w/up 400 8 x 100 @205R cooldown 200	45 min aerobic (75–85 rpm)	30 min aerobic
Wed	off	30 min aerobic (90+ rpm)	30 min aerobic
Thurs	w/up 500 8 x 50 drill choice @205R 5 x 100 free	w/up 10 min., 10 min tempo (TT effort), cooldown 20 min aerobic	off
Fri	w/up 300 20 x 50 drill choice @ 155R, cooldown	1.5 hrs aerobic	off
Sat	off	off	30 min aerobic
Sun	off	off	45 min aerobic

Aerobic Zones:

bike =   run =   Mon—bike 45 min aerobic (90+ rpm)

Tues—repeat last Tuesday

Tempo Zones: 80–90%

bike =   run =

that extra edge for your personal best by helping you plan, train, and exercise safely.

Success Story: Tom

Throughout middle school, Tom was told that he was big and fat. If he wasn't getting beaten up by the kids at school, he was running away from getting beaten up. During high school, all he heard was that he was fat, ugly, and slow. At five-foot-four and 250 pounds, he was overweight, but other people's low opinion of him and his own lack of self-esteem were about to change.

Tom was assigned to a physical education class for overweight kids and kids with problems or handicaps. Although the other kids in school continued to laugh at him for being in the "fat kids' gym class," one of his physical education teachers told the class, "If you work hard, you will all see results."

Tom was a master at finding excuses for getting out of gym class. But as time went on, the support and encouragement of that teacher started to make a difference. Tom could barely run a lap around the track without stopping to catch his breath. But each day he worked harder and harder, and the results started to show about six weeks into the class.

One day when Tom went to pick up the newspapers for his paper route, the supervisor at the office was yelling at the kids to hurry up and get their papers. Picking up his bag with one hundred newspapers in it was always difficult for Tom. But in that moment of haste, he grabbed the bag, threw it over his shoulder, and started to ride off. All of a sudden, he felt strong. His hard work was paying off.

Tom ran his first mile without stopping—something that had been inconceivable to him before. He started to eat better to lose weight. He was feeling great about himself. He even went out and about with friends on his skateboard. Tom was gaining control of his weight and his sense of self.

Almost three years and 130 pounds later, at the age of eighteen, Tom ran his first marathon. The support he had received from his gym teacher "granted him life," he says. He has now competed in more than 170 triathlons over the past eighteen years, including several Ironman distance races. He has even done the Eco-Challenge, has completed a 152-mile run in the Sahara, and has run a marathon in Antarctica.

CHAPTER 8

Get It in Writing: Keep a Log

For all of life is like that race,
With ups and downs and all.
And all you have to do to win
Is rise each time you fall.
"Quit! Give up, you're beaten!"
They still shout in my face.
But another voice within me says:
"Get up and win the race!"

—D. H. GROBERG

Training and Exercise Logs

One of the best tools to track and monitor your progress is a log or diary. Maintaining a log can discipline you to complete your workouts and will help you watch your eating habits. After all, the pages in the log don't lie—unless you do!

On the next page you'll see what a training log looks like. You need to have enough space each day to list what exercise, distance, or time you plan to do; what you actually do; your heart rate; how you felt; and any other comments. I use little faces to keep track of how I feel during each day's workout. How you feel, both physically and emotionally, is very important—and that doesn't always show up in mileage and heart rate figures.

Weekly Training Schedule			Weekly Training Results		Heart Rate Summary						Max/Min HR
Date	Sport	Time	Sport	Distance	A.M. RHR	Min/Max HR	Above	In	Below	Avg	Notes & Comments
Mon		Off		Off							☺ ☺ ☹
Tues	Swim		Swim								☺ ☺ ☹
	Cycle		Cycle								
	Run		Run								
Wed	Swim		Swim								☺ ☺ ☹
	Cycle		Cycle								
	Run		Run								
Thurs	Swim		Swim								☺ ☺ ☹
	Cycle		Cycle								
	Run		Run								
Fri	Swim		Swim								☺ ☺ ☹
	Cycle		Cycle								
	Run		Run								
Sat	Swim		Swim								☺ ☺ ☹
	Cycle		Cycle								
	Run		Run								
Sun	Swim		Swim								☺ ☺ ☹
	Cycle		Cycle								
	Run		Run								

Weekly Training Schedule Summary:

Swim Total _____ Bike Total _____ Run Total _____

RHR = Resting heart rate
Above = Time above maximum heart rate zone
In = Time in target heart rate zone
Below = Time below target heart rate zone
Avg = Average time in target zone

Weekly Review Goals/Notes:

☺ ☺ ☹

96

On the following page is what my first triathlon training log looked like. Notice that not all the days were good days, but gradually I had more good days than bad. Even the pros have bad days. The famous triathlete Mark Allen says that you should just try to get 100 percent out of yourself each day. In other words, do your best.

Log Guidelines

Here are a few simple guidelines to follow when making or buying a training log.

1 **Make it fun.** Think of making log entries as a fun thing to do. You don't have to be serious. In fact, the more fun you have, the more likely you are to do it. If you don't like to write, use a checklist or draw pictures. Just leave enough space for yourself, and make sure you'll understand what you meant when you look back at each page a year from now.

2 **Find a format or application that you will use every day.** You can keep any type of log you want. I used the computer to create a simple document with the table function. Then I printed out fifty-two copies and started filling them in week by week. You can look for preprinted planning pages or training logs and enlarge them on a copier. Make sure you have enough room for notes.

3 **Be creative.** You can be creative with the style, format, and information in your log. Try stickers, artwork, or photographs for the cover and inside. Add motivational quotes and poems you come across. Make it personal. This should be something you will enjoy writing in daily.

4 **Keep it simple.** For example, when I decided to stop worrying so much about losing weight and to start focusing on getting healthy, I started a training log. It's easy to see how I progressed. My first few logs (January 18 to February 7) included one entry a week for playing volleyball. Then I joined a step aer-

| Weekly Training Schedule | | | Weekly Training Results | | Heart Rate Summary | | | | | | Max/Min HR | |
Date	Sport	Time	Sport	Distance	A.M. RHR	Min/Max HR	Above	In	Below	Avg		Notes & Comments
Mon		Off		Off	52						☺☻☹ ☻☒	massage
Tues	Swim	swim	Swim	swim							☺☻☹ ☻☒	
	Cycle	1 hr	Cycle	1 hr								okay
	Run	a.m. 30 min	Run	run 30 min		148/105	00	:28	:02	144		
Wed	Swim	off	Swim	swim							☺☻☹ ☻☒	better day
	Cycle	2 hrs	Cycle	2 hrs 20 min								no swim
	Run	1 hr	Run	1 hr			00	:585	:0131	:150		
Thurs	Swim	off	Swim	off							☺☻☹ ☻☒	
	Cycle	3 hrs	Cycle	3 hrs 45 min		54/94	:00	:20	2:33	121		wasn't feeling the best
	Run	off	Run	off								
Fri	Swim	swim	Swim	off							☺☻☹ ☻☒	
	Cycle	off	Cycle	off								totally out of it!
	Run	1 hr easy	Run	20 min		146/84	:00	:07	1250	119		sucked!
Sat	Swim	off	Swim	off							⊛☻☹ ☻☒	good ride and eating
	Cycle	off	Cycle	6 hrs		184/84	:00	2329	3:20	134		properly helped
	Run	15 min easy	Run	45 min		171/134	:00	:453	:00	154		good new shoes helped too
Sun	Swim	didn't	Swim	1:50		140/22	:00	1828	136	120	☺☻☹ ☻☒	
	Cycle	race	Cycle	1:50 20/35								excellent run
	Run		Run	2:45		155/107	:00	2:10	3353	109		happy with myself

Weekly Training Schedule Summary:
Swim Total 4X   Bike Total 13:40   Run Total ____   Run Total 5:30

RHR = Resting heart rate
Above = Time above maximum heart rate zone
In = Time in target heart rate zone
Below = Time below target heart rate zone
Avg = Average time in target zone

Weekly Review Goals/Notes:
⊛☻☹

obics class. My first scheduled walk was on February 18. By March 3, I was able to jog an entire mile—fourteen laps on an indoor track without stopping. I had a big smiley face that day.

5 **Be honest.** Nobody's log is filled only with accomplishments. There will be bumps along the way—workouts missed due to work, travel, or sickness. Things happen. If you are having a bad day and don't work out, write it down anyway. I remember while training for the Hawaii Ironman in 1998, I was doing great up until Friday, August 28. On that date, I simply circled the frown face and wrote, "Sucked!" I added a side note that I was mentally out of it and cried. I used the rest of the evening to relax and refocus my energies on going out the next day and doing the best I could. On Saturday, August 29, I did six hours on the bike, followed by a forty-five-minute run.

6 **Schedule your exercise for the week.** If you exercise at regular times, you're less likely to miss a workout. Having a log helps get you off the couch. You need to have something to write down every day, which means you need to move your body every day. A log will help you start each week off with a plan and a schedule. Be flexible, though, as life won't necessarily follow your plan. Many times I've had a great week planned, only to find out I had to go out of town on business. You may have to adjust your plan temporarily, but your log will help you see that you're in this for the long haul.

7 **Make an effort to record every day and every workout in your log.** When I look back to August 11, 1996, there is a big smiley face for finishing my first triathlon. An unbelievable rush of emotion comes back when I look at that entry. I can see, hear, and feel all the events of that day, including crossing the finish line. But a notation for August 17, when I broke my foot, is haunting. During the emergency surgery, months in a cast, and physical therapy, the entries took on a different tone, a different meaning. I can see when I was able to return to exercising—it was very slow. I followed my doctor's recommendations for a return to my running program. By January 1, 1997, the log notes that I was able to complete one mile of jogging without any pain. That log is not just a list of workouts; it's the story of my life.

8 **Use the log as a tool to help keep you on track.** A log can be a valuable source of information. It can serve to remind you of what works and what doesn't. Periodically, look back over your old entries to keep yourself on the right track. This also serves as a reminder of how far you've come and as motivation to keep going. Your log will help you remember personal victories when you're feeling down and frustrated. Use the log to get personal and make the most of your accomplishments.

9 **Expand your log.** When I learned how valuable monitoring my morning heart rate could be, I added a column for that to my log. In fact, every time I got on the computer to print out more copies, I added more columns.

10 **Share your log with others.** Sometimes my coach made suggestions of things to include in my log to help him track my training and progress.

•

Soon my whole life was reflected in my workout log. I can look back and see that I finally reached my goal of running 26.2 miles on January 11, 1998, at the Disney World Marathon. I set out to achieve that goal in 1996. I can see where I started and what it took to get to the finish line, and I can take pride in every step of the way.

A Log You Will Use

You can find logs for various sports in many bookstores. You can even buy a journal in which to keep your log. I use a three-ring binder to hold my log. A simple spiral notebook can work, too. Find something that is easy to carry with you and that you don't need to spend a lot of money on.

You also can purchase software to create an exercise log on the computer. In the Resources section, I list several programs that can help you personalize your plan for that first 5K race or marathon—or even a triathlon.

Even when I use a computer program, I still like to have a written copy of my log with me. Many times when I travel for work, I take my training log with me on the plane to review my heart rate information and record it. The covers of my annual training logs are bright pink and have graphics and photographs on them. Thanks to my friend and designer Tony Kause, I'm proud to carry my logs anywhere.

I still prefer to write in the information by hand. I do use a Polar interface to download my heart rate readings directly from my monitor to the computer for very detailed heart rate training information. I have just started using this, and it's fun. The software can com-

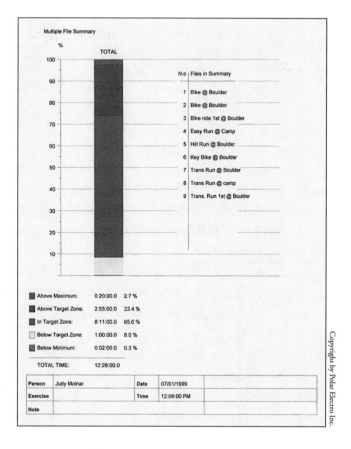

pile charts and reports of each week of training. (See Chapter 9 on heart rate training.) Above is a report from my week at the Multisport School of Champions Ironman training camp.

The key to keeping a log is to find a format or application that you will use. It is no good to set up a log if you won't use it every day to help schedule your exercise routines and track your progress.

Food Logs

Keeping a food log in addition to an exercise log can help you stay on track with your eating. With a food journal, you can monitor exactly what and how much you eat.

When I started out, my nutritionist suggested that I keep a food log for two weeks to determine when, what, how much, and why I was eating. This was a great tool to help me learn about eating and start additional planning.

Keeping a food log is as simple as writing down what you eat for breakfast, lunch, dinner, and snacks every day. Make sure not to censor yourself, because this is an opportunity to take a look at your eating patterns and work on them. Also try to figure out how much you eat. Portions can be very deceiving. If you are putting several cups of pasta or a few chicken breasts on your plate, you are eating too much of even healthy foods.

In Chapters 12 and 13, you will find some basic nutrition information that will help you fill your food log (and your body) with healthy choices in the right portions.

Nutritional Chart for the Week of _____

	Monday	Tuesday	Wednesday	Thursday	Friday	Saturday	Sunday
BREAKFAST	Time _____	Time _____	Time _____	Time _____	Time _____	Time _____	Time _____
A.M. SNACK							
LUNCH	Time _____	Time _____	Time _____	Time _____	Time _____	Time _____	Time _____
P.M. SNACK							
DINNER	Time _____	Time _____	Time _____	Time _____	Time _____	Time _____	Time _____
TOTAL CALORIES & FAT							

CHAPTER 9

Listen to Your Heart: Heart Rate Training

The way you prepare has more to do with your success than any amount of luck you might experience.

—JOE MONTANA

A few years ago, the Polar Heart Rate Monitor became one of the keys to my success in losing weight. I was learning to work out in my heart rate target zone (TZ)—exercising more slowly and for a longer time. Guess what? You burn more fat when you do that! I also believe that this kind of training helped take me from 5K runs to marathons to doing triathlons.

Watching my heart rate was fun. It became the coach at my side and an awesome tool to monitor my progress. When I was going too hard and too fast, it beeped at me. When I was slacking off, it also beeped. That is one of the great features of training with a heart rate monitor—it is easy to see or hear when you're in (or out) of your TZ.

For the technical stuff, I've asked the experts at Polar to explain why your heart rate is so important and how their monitor works. All I can say is, get one!

From the Folks at Polar

No matter who you are—Olympic athlete, weekend warrior, or someone trying to get started on an exercise program to lose weight—a heart rate monitor can play an important role. It takes the guesswork out of exercise by letting you know exactly how hard you are working out.

Your heart is the most important muscle you have. It serves as a barometer for the rest of your body, telling you how hard you are exercising, how fast you are using up energy, and even your emotional state. And it does all this instantly and continuously. Your heart will tell you if you are exercising too lightly or dangerously overexerting yourself. A heart rate monitor is like your own personal coach, right on your wrist, guiding you through your workout.

The key to effective exercise is working out at the right intensity. If you exercise too lightly, you get very few benefits from the time you put in. In today's world, when workouts need to fit into a busy schedule, you want to make sure you get the most benefit from the time that you have to exercise. By contrast, people who work out too hard feel unnecessary pain and discomfort and often quit because it hurts or because they injure themselves. If you work out too hard, you also go from aerobic to anaerobic mode and stop burning fat for energy. Exercising too long or too often in anaerobic mode can actually impair your fat-burning system. The heart rate monitor will pace you so that you can complete your workout at the level that will give you the most benefit. The days of "no pain, no gain" are over.

The heart rate range that is right for your exercise is based on your age and fitness level. This is referred to as the heart rate target zone (TZ). If you're fifty-eight, you shouldn't be working out at the same level as someone who is twenty-one. You can find your TZ by using a chart provided with the monitor or by doing a simple computation.

The heart rate monitor also can provide some other valuable information that you can't get any other way. It can tell you if you are dehydrating during exercise. It can tell you if you are tired from a hard workout that you did yesterday or if an illness is coming on. These tidbits of information will allow you to modify your exercise for each day.

If you have not fully recovered from a hard workout yesterday and you are expecting to do another hard workout today, you risk injury or burnout. You may have high expectations for today's workout (add ten minutes to your run, for example). If you cannot reach that goal, you get frustrated. If you know that you're still a little tired from yesterday, you can be more realistic about what you should try to do today. If you didn't have a heart rate monitor on, you wouldn't have this perspective.

Your body can provide you with very important information if you choose to listen to it. You want to see results from your exercise. What are results? Loss of weight, a toned body, and better fitness. If you don't see results, you get frustrated, miss workouts, and maybe even quit.

Results take time. It may be a few weeks before you see a difference on the scale. Sometimes you have to get more aerobically fit before you see the weight start to roll off. That's the first step. But how can you tell you're getting more aerobically fit? Use a heart rate monitor. As you get fit, you will see changes in your heart rate. This is a sign that your body is benefiting from exercise. When you see those changes, you are more likely to stay with the program so that you can eventually see the weight coming off. That's motivation!

How Does a Heart Rate Monitor Work?

A heart rate monitor is a two-piece system that is easy to use. The first piece is a transmitter that you wear on your chest. It's very flexible and is attached with an elastic strap that holds it comfortably in place. The better heart rate monitors are waterproof, so you can wear them while swimming.

The transmitter picks up your heart's signal and sends it to a wrist receiver that looks like a watch. All you have to do is look at your wrist and watch the numbers change as you go through your workout. Some models allow you to set your TZ, and if you are exercising outside your TZ, it will alert you with an audible alarm. On simpler models, you can just keep an eye on the numbers and slow down a little when you get to the top of your TZ or speed up if you drop below it.

With a heart rate monitor, you know right away if you're slacking off or working too hard, and you can adjust your pace accordingly.

A wireless heart rate monitor gives you the same accuracy as an electrocardiogram (EKG) and doesn't restrict you from performing any type of activity.

Why can't you just take your pulse and do the math? First, the process of taking your pulse is not very convenient. You have to find the carotid artery in your neck. Once you find it, you look at your watch and count to ten. Then you solve a multiplication problem and come up with your beats per minute (bpm). That might be doable while you're standing still, but try doing it while you are exercising!

Monitoring your heart rate *during* exercise is the key to success. With a heart rate monitor, you just look at the receiver on your wrist, and all the information you need is displayed for you.

If you are getting fitter, your heart rate is going to get more efficient and start to drop as soon as you stop exercising. If you stop to take your pulse for ten seconds, you are going to get a lower reading than taking it while you are exercising. It is also very difficult to count your heartbeats accurately when your heart rate is elevated. If you are off as little as five beats, it could mean the difference between being in your TZ and being above it.

There are other ways to measure your heart rate, such as taking your pulse at your wrist or earlobe or using a finger clip. Accuracy is an issue with these methods, however.

Which Monitor?

The first step is to purchase a heart rate monitor. Several manufacturers offer different models, but the market leader is Polar Electro, the company that actually invented the heart rate monitor more than twenty years ago. Polar monitors are still the most popular choice among athletes and fitness enthusiasts around the world. Several models are available, with a starting price of fifty dollars, as well as more expensive models with features designed for athletes in specific sports.

All the Polar units are EKG accurate and waterproof. You can start with the entry-level product (Beat), which is easy to use and has large numbers for easy viewing.

The key when purchasing a unit is to buy the model that is right for you. Perhaps the most valuable feature for a beginner is found in the Target model, which allows you to set a TZ and which sounds an alarm when you exercise out of the TZ. This lets you focus on your exercise as the unit guides your actions.

The Pacer tells you how long you have exercised and how much of that time you have spent in your TZ.

While getting healthy is a serious business, it's good to keep your sense of humor. Lauri Levenfeld, Zoom Photography, California

Remember, that's your fat-burning exercise time. The next model, the M21, actually counts calories, automatically assesses your fitness, and picks a TZ for you to work in each day. The M52 has a fitness test that evaluates your fitness while you are standing still. Models such as the Coach and Accurex Plus download your heart rate data to a personal computer so that you can keep a training log and do advanced analysis.

For more information, you can visit Polar's website at www.polarusa.com or call (800) 227-1314.

What Is Your Target Zone?

Once you have your heart rate monitor, the next step is to establish your TZ and workout numbers. The best way to do this is to have your doctor do a stress test. This is especially recommended if you are just starting an exercise program or have been sedentary for a while.

Another method is to use formulas based on scientific research. The most popular formula allows you to establish your estimated maximum heart rate and then take percentages of that number to establish your TZ. (The Polar website has a heart rate counter. You just type in your age, and it will tell you your maximum heart rate and your TZ.) For instance, 60 to 70 percent of maximum heart rate is a good zone for someone just starting out or trying to build up his or her endurance. Here's an example using that range:

220 − 34 (your age) = 186 (estimated maximum heart rate)

186 × .60 = 112 (60% of maximum heart rate)

186 × .70 = 130 (70% of maximum heart rate)

Based on these calculations, the starting TZ for this person would be 112 to 130 bpm.

If you wanted to find the next TZ, or an intensity level of 70 to 80 percent of maximum heart rate, multiply 186 by .70 and .80.

The next method takes into consideration your fitness level. There's a big difference between a fit, healthy thirty-four-year-old and a thirty-four-year-old who is thirty pounds overweight and doesn't exercise. You can personalize your numbers by factoring in your morning resting heart rate (MRHR). When you first wake up, your body is at its most rested, and your MRHR is a good indicator of your fitness level. For example, for someone 34 years old with an MRHR of 63, the calculations are as follows:

220 − 34 = 186

186 − 63 = 123

123 × .60 = 74

123 × .70 = 86

Then you add your MRHR back in:

74 + 63 = 137

86 + 63 = 149

The TZ for this person is 137 to 149 bpm. This is higher than the calculation that did not factor in the resting heart rate (112 to 130 bpm).

Professional athletes usually have their numbers determined through scientific testing at a sports clinic. This is not necessary for the everyday athlete or fitness enthusiast. No matter what your goals, however, a heart rate monitor can be an important element of your exercise program.

The Importance of Staying in Your Target Zone

There are two types of exercise—aerobic and anaerobic. The difference between the two has to do with where you get the energy to move your muscles. In an aerobic workout, you're burning mostly fat. In an anaerobic workout, you're burning mostly carbohydrates. Oddly enough, the aerobic workout requires a lower heart rate.

If you're trying to lose weight, you need to be careful to stay in that fat-burning zone. Working out too hard can actually switch your system out of the fat-burning mode. If you've been working out for months and show no loss of weight and no significant reshaping of your body, this could be your problem.

Working out in your TZ ensures that you're burning fat while gaining fitness. It also lets you work out longer, because you have a lot of energy stored in fat.

Success Story: Brandi

"You've been dead for seventeen minutes," Brandi, age twenty-five, hears as she awakens from open-heart surgery.

Brandi was eighteen years old when she was diagnosed with a debilitating cardiac dysrhythmia. She was forced to quit her college track team and told she could no longer compete in sports. But that was the least of her worries. For Brandi, simply climbing a flight of stairs without passing out became a challenge.

Over the next seven years, Brandi underwent seven heart surgeries. Her journey through these surgeries was demoralizing. One doctor, she said, told her to resign herself to the condition. Another said she'd grow out of it. "Why don't you just go and see a psychiatrist and deal with having a dormant lifestyle?" she says he told her. "Basically, he wanted me to be a one-hundred-year-old person when I was in my twenties."

On December 15, 1997, she had a permanent atrial pacemaker implanted. It was during this procedure that she was clinically dead for seventeen minutes. Miraculously, two weeks later she began running, something she had not done since she was diagnosed with the dysrhythmia.

Brandi has started a new life by taking control of her health and exercise and by aggressively pursuing research and information on her condition. She is swimming, biking, and running like never before. In August 1998, she rode fourteen hundred miles from St. Louis, Missouri, to Orlando, Florida, to raise money for chiropractic research.

"I feel fortunate that, after everything I've been through, I can go back to leading a normal life," Brandi says. "A few years ago, walking around the block was extremely difficult, and now I can run for hours at a time. Since I train with a Polar Heart Rate Monitor, I know exactly how hard I'm working, and I don't have to worry about my heart rate jumping to a dangerous level."

Brandi's improvement has been so remarkable that her doctors have published parts of her medical file in a cardiology journal. In addition, she now requires a more technologically advanced pacemaker to keep up with her endurance level.

Brandi is at the point where she is once again able to participate in athletic competitions. She plans to continue to race in triathlons and road races. Her dream is to compete in the Hawaii Ironman. With everything that Brandi has overcome, it seems that there is nothing she can't accomplish.

CHAPTER 10

Cross-Trainer Is Not Just a Shoe Design

The world is not interested in the storms you encountered but did you bring in the ship.

—WILLIAM MCFEE

After my initial commitment to walking and running, I found myself getting bored with the same workout day in and day out. Finding a few activities that I could combine into a program solved part of that problem. Cross-training is simply doing more than one type of exercise. My triathlon coach, Troy Jacobson, told me, "Cross-training is the ideal way to achieve optimal total body fitness. With cross-training, you get the best of all worlds, including muscular conditioning, increased cardiovascular fitness, body fat loss, variety in training, reduced risk of overuse injuries, and more!"

I always focused on races to give me motivation. My ultimate goal was to run a marathon. I knew that amount of running would be tough on me due to my weight. So I started out slowly, with a goal of running a 5K. I knew that, as the weight came off, I could continue to increase my running miles. But I also found that I tended to get bored quickly with doing the same exercise over and over. And

I have to remember to pace myself. It's not going to happen instantly. It's taking me more time than I thought it would to even get these shoes on.

Lauri Levenfeld, Zoom Photography, California

after a while, I didn't need to gear up for a 5K anymore. When I started aiming at a 10K, it was more of the same thing.

Then I heard about a local triathlon, and I thought, "This is exactly what I need!" I thought of it as cross-training that included swimming, biking, and running. I didn't wake up one morning and say, "I am going to do triathlon races." But over months of getting in shape, I found myself able to take on various fitness activities. I wanted to see what I could do and not be tied to what other people thought I *couldn't* do because of my size.

I even incorporated cross-training into a strength-training routine. I would life a few sets, then get on the treadmill for a short run, go back to another strength exercise, and get on the bike to spin a bit. This made the time go faster. My trainer at the gym helped me learn the importance of cross-training with aerobic exercises while lifting weights.

A Side Note

The "no pain, no gain" theory went out of fashion a long time ago. Exercise is not about pain but about doing it safely and feeling strong. Don't do so much, so hard, so fast that you get hurt and can't work out anymore. Cross-training will help you avoid overuse injuries, get you moving more, and keep your routine fresh. But you still have to pay attention to your body. Don't push it further than it's ready to go. If you have any questions or concerns about your fitness activities, talk to your doctor. Get a complete physical every year. Remember, this is about becoming healthy. That means working with your doctor and following his or her orders to minimize any health risks and to take care of any injuries right away.

Where do you look for cross-training activities? Just take a look at this short list of possibilities: aerobics, ballet or any other kind of dance, yoga, swimming, biking, running, tennis, golf, water aerobics, cross-country skiing, walking, hiking, climbing, martial arts, racquetball, rowing, volleyball, skating, squash, snowboarding. That's just the tip of the iceberg. Anything that gets your body moving counts, and the more different groups of muscles you can use, the better.

The key is to be creative with the activities you participate in. Take the time to try a few different ones and find several that you enjoy. Try a few that you never thought you could do—you might be surprised. And then, throughout each week, mix them up.

In the beginning, I tried all kinds of activities—volleyball, basketball, step machines, yoga, rowing machines, aerobics classes, golfing—looking for the ones I liked best. While I was doing all this sampling, I was moving more in a lot of different ways.

I really enjoyed the step aerobics class because of the music. Yoga was great for stretching, but I had to get over the mystical stuff. I'd enjoyed running before, so I started walking with a view toward advancing to running when I could. The stationary bike gave me a new idea for moving more. I liked the idea of taking the pressure off my joints, and cycling did that. I don't think I ever found an activity I didn't like, except maybe chin-ups, dips, and push-ups, because I just couldn't do them.

One thing I thought I was going to hate was swimming. I was dreading the thought of wearing a swimsuit. I didn't even own one. Also, I had not swum since I was a kid. I thought swimming was something I had to do because it is part of triathlons.

Even though I barely made twenty-five yards in my first workout, there was something soothing about the water. It was so refreshing, and my body seemed to move through it without any pressure or stress. I always felt relaxed after swimming, even though it took a lot out of me to do those laps.

So don't be scared to try something you haven't done before or think you can't do. With practice and instruction, you can do it.

Success Story: Bill

A typical day for Bill in his Palm Desert, California, home begins with a thousand repetitions on a rowing machine, followed by a light breakfast and a brisk one-mile swim, twenty-mile bike ride, or ten-mile run. He also adds strength training to his routine. Afternoons are for something "wimpy" like golf.

Bill is a seventeen-time Hawaii Ironman veteran and has completed close to four hundred endurance events such as marathons, triathlons, and cycling races. He even participated in the Race Across America (RAAM), considered the world's toughest endurance event. It's a three-thousand-mile race across the United States from the West Coast to the East Coast.

Oh, by the way, Bill is seventy-six years old!

But Bill wasn't always into exercise and pushing his body to the limits of his endurance. During a military entrance exam in 1942, he was diagnosed with an irregular heartbeat, which prevented him from serving in World War II and sidelined him for any physical activity. But medical research and information changed over the years, and when Bill was in his fifties, his doctor advised him to start an exercise routine that included light jogging, bicycling, or swimming three days a week.

"I felt so good I did it every day for two hours," Bill says. A year later, he started running marathons.

"God gave me this wonderful body," he says. "You can get parts for it, but you can't get a new one. I want to use mine as well as I can, while I still can."

CHAPTER 11

Workouts

*Success is a peace of mind, which is a direct result of
self-satisfaction in knowing you did your best to
become the best that you are capable of becoming.*

—JOHN WOODEN

Before You Start

I strongly recommend these steps before you start, or even restart, any exercise program.

1 **GO TO A DOCTOR TO GET A PHYSICAL CHECKUP.** They say in E-mail that typing in all caps is considered yelling. Guess what? I'm yelling this at the top of my lungs. I can't emphasize enough how important it is to see a doctor when you are gearing up to exercise. I know that going to a doctor's office means stepping on a scale, but it is something you must do. Starting an exercise program without visiting a doctor can lead to injury and unnecessary health risks. This can be especially true if you are overweight.

2 Hire a coach or personal trainer, talk to the fitness staff at your local health club, or join a running group or masters swim class. Find people and resources that will help you learn how you can get moving more. Don't be shy about asking questions.

3 Find someone to do it with. Don't use the excuse "I don't have anyone." Check out local running, walking, and exercise groups. You will be surprised at how many people have the same goals and interests. For listings of every kind of fitness club you can imagine, check out the Active USA website, activeusa.com.

Eight-Week 5K Training Program for Beginners

People always ask me, "How do I start a training program?" When I started, I went straight to the pages of sports-related magazines and books to find training plans for running. I set up my first workouts myself after getting a physical checkup and talking to my doctor about what I could realistically demand of my already-overworked heart.

You will be amazed at what you'll find if you start educating yourself and being proactive about your activities. There is a tremendous amount of information, resources, and fitness professionals out there to help you accomplish your personal goals.

5K WORKOUT TRAINING PROGRAM

Weeks 1 and 2 (Initiation Phase)

Day	Workout	Other Training
1	15 min brisk walk	
	(jog easy for 1 min once every 5 min)	
2	Off	Circuit weight training*

*Circuit weight training is something you can do to help build your lean muscle mass. A simple routine can be going through one series of the weight machines for upper and lower body strength at the gym.

3	20 min brisk walk	
	(jog easy for 1 min once every 5 min)	
4	Off	
5	30 min brisk walk	
	(jog easy for 1 min once every 5 min)	
6	Off	Circuit weight training
7	Off	

Weeks 3 and 4 (Building Phase I)

Day	Workout	Other Training
1	20 min brisk walk	
	(jog easy for 2 min once every 5 min)	
2	Off	Circuit weight training
3	30 min brisk walk	
	(jog easy for 2 min once every 5 min)	
4	Off	
5	30 min brisk walk	
	(jog easy for 2 min once every 5 min)	
6	Off	Circuit weight training
7	40 min brisk walk	

Weeks 5 and 6 (Building Phase II)

Day	Workout	Other Training
1	30 min brisk walk	
	(jog easy for 3 min once every 5 min)	
2	Off	Circuit weight training
3	30 min brisk walk	
	(jog easy for 3 min once every 5 min)	
4	Off	
5	30 min brisk walk	
	(jog easy for 3 min once every 5 min)	
6	Off	Circuit weight training
7	50 min brisk walk	

Week 7 (Race Simulation Phase)

Day	Workout	Other Training
1	40 min jog (walk 1 min once every 5 min)	
2	Off	Circuit weight training
3	30 min jog (walk only if necessary)	
4	Off	
5	60 min brisk walk	
6	Off	Circuit weight training
7	Off	

Week 8 (Taper)

Day	Workout	Other Training
1	30 min jog (jog 1 min/walk 1 min)	
2	Off	Circuit weight training
3	20 min brisk walk (jog easy for 1 min once every 5 min)	
4	Off	
5	Off	
6	15 min brisk walk	Light stretching
7	5K race! Good luck!	

Swimming and biking are great alternative options for other training.

Make sure you include rest in your workout schedule. It's a very important part of any kind of training. Get plenty of sleep and take at least one day off every week. Rest time is when your muscles actually get a chance to repair themselves and get stronger. And don't start this or any workout program until you've cleared it with your doctor.

Twelve-Week Marathon Training Program for Beginners

This twelve-week program is for the first-time marathoner. The objective is to help you finish the 26.2-mile event using a steady but modest pace. Speed is not a concern. However, you will occasionally do "tempo" running to increase your running efficiency, improve your cardiovascular fitness, and develop a sense of pace. Anyone preparing for a marathon should have at least three months of general fitness training (including strength training, running, and other cardiovascular conditioning exercises), as well as the ability to complete a 10K race, before beginning this twelve-week program.

This workout plan uses time and intensity instead of miles. By using time and intensity, you can control your efforts more effectively, as well as monitor your progress. Using a heart rate monitor is recommended (determine your target zone by using the formula provided with the monitor or by being tested), but it is not required. Aerobic training is to be done at a comfortable "talking" pace. Tempo training is to be done at a pace that is slightly uncomfortable yet sustainable.

The entire time specified (for example, "45 min aerobic") should be done at the aerobic intensity, including a warm-up and cooldown. The "tempo" efforts (for example, 45 min aerobic [10 min tempo]) should be done midway through the aerobic exercise.

Since the goal of this program is to enable you to finish a marathon, it is recommended that you incorporate walk breaks into the longer training days. These breaks can be scheduled (1 minute walk for every 10 minutes of running) or random (whenever it is necessary).

MARATHON TRAINING PROGRAM

Week	Mon	Tues	Wed	Thurs	Fri	Sat	Sun
1	Off	30 min aerobic	40 min aerobic	Off	45 min aerobic	Off	1 hr aerobic
2	Off	30 min aerobic	45 min aerobic	Off	45 min aerobic	Off	1 hr aerobic

Week	Mon	Tues	Wed	Thurs	Fri	Sat	Sun
3	Off	40 min aerobic (5 min tempo)	1 hr aerobic	Off	45 min aerobic	30 min aerobic or off	1.5 hr aerobic
4	Off	45 min aerobic (8 min tempo)	1 hr aerobic	Off	45 min aerobic	30 min aerobic	1.5 hr aerobic
5	Off	45 min aerobic (8 min tempo)	1 hr aerobic	Off	1 hr aerobic	Off	2 hr aerobic
6	Off	45 min aerobic (10 min tempo)	1 hr aerobic	Off	1 hr aerobic	30 min aerobic	2.5 hr aerobic
7	Off	1 hr aerobic (10 min tempo)	1 hr aerobic	Off	1 hr aerobic	30 min aerobic	3 hr aerobic
8	Off	1 hr aerobic (10 min tempo)	1 hr aerobic	Off	1 hr aerobic	Off	2.5 hr aerobic
9	Off	45 min aerobic (5 min tempo)	45 min aerobic	Off	1 hr aerobic	30 min aerobic	2 hr aerobic
10	Off	40 min aerobic (5 min tempo)	45 min aerobic	Off	45 min aerobic	Off	1.5 hr aerobic

Week	Mon	Tues	Wed	Thurs	Fri	Sat	Sun
11	Off	30 min aerobic	45 min aerobic	Off	30 min aerobic	Off	1 hr aerobic
12	Off	30 min easy	Off	20 min easy	Off	15 min easy	Race!

My Marathon Story

For my first marathon, I chose to do the Walt Disney World Marathon in Orlando, Florida. I actually trained for it twice, but a broken foot in August 1996 ended my shot for the 1997 race. The January 1998 event was a different case.

To prepare for the marathon, I built up my fitness base all year with triathlons, road races, and cycling. The marathon was the next distance for me to conquer.

I trained patiently and consistently throughout the fall and early winter of 1997. Training for a January marathon is tough in the Midwest, but with planning and warm clothing, you can run pretty much anytime.

I will never forget a thirteen-mile run I did with my boyfriend, Rick, in November, however. It was below thirty degrees Fahrenheit, and snow was on the ground. We kept moving forward, trying to stay warm. As we hit the final two miles or so, we walked through the mall because the cold was getting to us. That was a big mistake because we still had to go outside to finish. My legs started to cramp up, and I remember thinking, "Orlando in January is going to be a major relief."

Unfortunately, I had another little incident during the final weeks of training that almost prevented me from racing. Rick and I had gone to his hometown for the holidays. He went swimming, and I went for a run. I headed out through the town and was running well. I made a decision as I hit the country road to run on the more populated side. In front of a farmhouse, eight dogs came charging at me from the front lawn. I was yelling at them to stop, and some scurried away. But a Great Dane was biting my hand, and another dog was trying to bite my calf. I continued to run faster as the owner called most of the dogs off. One stayed with me, though, and bit through my tights and into my left calf. I was bleeding, scared, and crying a bit. I asked the owner about the dog, but he said he didn't know anything about its shots. I was so distressed by the blood and the owner's harsh reaction that I just took off running. I couldn't believe how fast my heart was racing. I probably ran the fastest five miles of my life heading back home.

When I got back to the house, Rick's family insisted that I go to the doctor to have it checked out. The doctor said that there was no way I could run a marathon in two weeks. I was completely depressed, but I continued to clean and monitor the wound. When I got home, my doctor checked it out and gave me a clean bill of health.

On January 8, I left for Florida alone, because Rick and the rest of my support group couldn't get off work. This was a journey I needed to complete by myself anyway. It was truly a dream come true to be at Walt Disney World. I even loved the theme of the marathon, which was "Go the Distance" from *Hercules*. The song had become my training mantra.

The night before the race, my whole experience of setting goals and following dreams came together. At Disney World, they have a turndown service, where they place little cards and candy on the pillows. No candy for me, but the cards always had some great quotes from Disney movies. The card on January 9 said, "The dreams you do dream really do come true." I started to cry. I called Rick, my mom and dad, and my sister, Jeanne, to share the quote. I was filled with joy and hope.

On January 10, 1998, at 6:00 A.M., the gun sounded and off we went on our marathon journey. It was great to be running early because the heat wasn't so bad. It also was still dark, so I didn't realize fully what was going on. My friend Jennifer Wise had suggested that I count the Mickey Mouse ears that I saw along the route. The park also provided lots of other distractions along the way. We ran through Cinderella Castle, and I even stopped a few times to take photos with the characters.

As I approached the finish line, I was smiling and crying. I couldn't believe that I had made it. There to greet me were Mickey Mouse and Minnie

Mouse. They placed my finisher's medal—shaped like Mickey's ears—around my neck. It was the best finisher's medal I had ever received.

When I got back to the room, I called everyone. I was on top of the world!

Just because the world says no doesn't mean you can't do something. Always reach for a goal that is a little outside your comfort zone. You will be surprised by the results.

Eight-Week Sprint Triathlon Training Program for Beginners

I know, I know. This is way more than you're ready for right now. I just want you to see what a training schedule looks like and the kind of training it takes to do a triathlon. The following program is for a sprint triathlon (.5 mile swimming, 12.5 mile biking, 3.1 mile running). Look at this again after you've been working out regularly for six months. It won't look nearly so impossible then—I guarantee it.

When you ride a bike, size becomes immaterial. I love exploring—the wind on my face, and the feeling of speed. Lauri Levenfeld, Zoom Photography, California

That was some cold water!

SPRINT TRIATHLON TRAINING PROGRAM

Weeks 1 and 2

Day	Swim	Bike	Run
Sun	Off	Off	40 min easy
Mon	Off	Off	Off
Tues	Off	30 min easy	30 min easy
Wed	Yes	Off	Off
Thurs	Off	45 min easy	Off
Fri	Off	Off	40 min easy
Sat	Yes	1 hr easy	Off

Weeks 3 and 4

Day	Swim	Bike	Run
Sun	Off	Off	45 min easy
Mon	Off	Off	Off
Tues	Off	30 min easy	40 min easy
Wed	Yes	Off	Off
Thurs	Yes	1 hr easy	Off
Fri	Off	Off	45 min easy
Sat	Off	1.5 hr easy	Off

Weeks 5 and 6

Day	Swim	Bike	Run
Sun	Off	Off	1 hr easy
Mon	Off	Off	Off
Tues	Off	30 min easy	45 min easy
Wed	Yes	45 min easy, rest 5 min	30 min easy (brisk workout)
Thurs	Yes	1 hr easy	Off
Fri	Off	Off	45 min easy
Sat	Off	1 hr easy, rest 5 min	30 min easy

Week 7

Day	Swim	Bike	Run
Sun	Off	Off	1 hr easy
Mon	Off	Off	Off
Tues	Off	1 hr easy	45 min easy
Wed	Yes	1 hr easy, rest 5 min	30 min easy
Thurs	Yes	1 hr easy	Off
Fri	Off	Off	30 min easy
Sat	Off	1 hr easy	Off

Week 8 (Taper)

Day	Swim	Bike	Run
Sun	Off	Off	40 min easy
Mon	Off	Off	Off
Tues	Off	30 min easy, rest 5 min	15 min easy
Wed	Yes	Off	Off
Thurs	Off	30 min easy bike	Off
Fri	Off	Off	15 min easy jog
Sat	Race!	Race!	Race!

Running in my first marathon.

Walt Disney World

Finishing the Schu triathlon for the second time!

CHAPTER 12

Why You Eat

Everyone thinks of changing the world, but no one thinks of changing himself.

—LEO TOLSTOY

No matter how much you move your body, to be really healthy, you're going to have to change the way you eat. You can do it gradually, but you just have to do it.

The turning point in my relationship with food was when I saw this flyer: "Get Control of Your Weight and Well-Being." Evelyn Cole-Kissinger, a registered dietitian and nutritionist, was conducting an eight-week class on nutrition and getting healthy. I signed up right away and made a commitment to attend every meeting. I learned so much about nutrition—reading labels, emotions and eating (a biggie for me), handling stress, cravings, what food really is, what a portion is, and how I could incorporate healthier habits into my diet. I highly recommend that you find a nutritionist to help you learn to apply the principles of good eating to your life. Face it, if you could do that without help, you probably wouldn't be reading this book.

Remember, there's nothing wrong with getting help. And a good nutritionist—in a class or a personal consultation—can help you understand your body and your relationship with food, manage your diet as your body changes with exercise, and show you ways to work good nutrition into your schedule and lifestyle. The American Dietetic Association has an online registry of nutritionists at www.eatright.org. You just type in your zip code to find a qualified professional near you. Or call the association's toll-free number, (800) 366-1655.

It's also a great idea to get the support of a wellness group. My classmates in the wellness group gave me a lot of feedback, tips, and advice. I wasn't alone in my struggle against bad habits and ignorance. Together, we learned to stop thinking "diet" and start thinking "healthier lifestyle."

Dealing with the Weight Issue

Why you eat is often overlooked when dealing with your weight. I used food as a source of comfort, whether I was bored, happy, or frustrated. Food was a good *temporary* stress reliever, but then came even more physical and emotional stress caused by my excess weight.

It helps to take a step back and examine how you make decisions. In my wellness class, we were asked to determine whether we were making choices out of pain or pleasure. To find this out for yourself, ask yourself these questions:

- Why do I eat?
- Why do I want to reach my healthy weight?
- What's keeping me from reaching my healthy weight?

When I first answered these questions, I was scared to be honest. But since I didn't have to show my answers to anyone, I could write the truth without fear of rejection. Here are the notes I took in class that day.

Why do I eat?

Well, I think out of habit, boredom, frustration, stress, and the need to escape. Food is my comfort at times.

Why do I want to reach my healthy weight?

Because I need to get control of my life and health and to find balance with my weight and who I am. Also to help with my self-esteem.

What's keeping me from reaching my healthy weight?

No discipline, unhappy with my life right now, no control, fear of failure again, and not being able to stay with it.

It's not fun to face your fears and behaviors when it comes to weight. But it is an important step in the process of achieving a healthy weight.

I learned to develop a new strategy and attitude about my weight. Some of the worst things I had to deal with were hopelessness, giving up, and not really caring. Then I was on the way to self-managed behavior. I am now in charge of my health. I never worried about my health because I was okay except for the weight. I had no problems with diabetes, high blood pressure, or high cholesterol. I had a chance to do something about my health before it was too late.

In my wellness class, we looked at weight and tried to identify both the positives and the negatives associated with it. I remember we all laughed at the "good" things about being overweight: being jollier, being warmer, being able to float, having more to love, knowing food and loving to eat, being less likely to starve on a desert island. But this discussion got us to start thinking about the positive things in our lives that weren't related to weight. This was a way to find new self-esteem and self-care. I started to realize that my whole life wasn't about weight. I had a lot going for me: my performance at work, volunteering, my talent in the theater, and more.

It takes time to accept that we aren't all meant to be the same size. Many of us blame the media for what we think of as the ideal body image. But it all comes down to self-awareness and self-acceptance. I know I will never be a size 2 or petite. I have a large frame and am over six feet tall. I am a bit hippy and have large thighs. I can't change that. So what?

Getting from what you think or others think your body should be to an acceptance of what you are is a long journey. It starts by recognizing that you pay a price in terms of the past, present, and future in relation to appearance, relationships (family, friends, significant other), social life, and health. In class, we received a chart to fill out with our thoughts about what effect weight has on these things.

	Past	Present	Future
Appearance			
Relationships			
Family			
Friends			
Significant other			
Social life			
Health			

As I went through this exercise, I found that my future was dark when it came to my health. I knew that in the past my denial of weight gain had gotten in my way. I always figured that big was beautiful and different was okay. But in the present I knew that appearance was one thing and health was another. There had to be a balance—a balance I was actively seeking for the first time in my life. I knew that there were changes I could make to see the future as bright and hopeful. You can, too. Sure, the past is full of issues, excuses, and events that made your weight an issue in the first place. But what is happening now? What can you take charge of?

The Emotions of Eating

If food is tied up with your emotions, how does that relationship work for you? How does it harm you? Here are some ideas to help you in this discovery process.

1 **Increase your awareness.** Become aware of food by keeping a diary, noting when you eat, what you eat, how much you eat, and the emotions you experience before, during, and after you eat (see Chapter 8). I found this to be enormously helpful—not only in learning about nutrition and eating right throughout the day, but in discovering the roadblocks to healthy eating and the triggers for overeating.

Start looking at the emotions that trigger your eating. Are you feeling angry, annoyed, bitter, bored, confused, disturbed, empty, envious, fearful, foolish, frustrated, full of grief or hate, guilty, happy, helpless, hurt, joyous, left out, lonely, miserable, nervous, obsessed, overwhelmed, in pain, pressured, rejected, rewarded, sad, stupid, ugly, or worried? I'm sure you can add many other emotions to this list. The key is to make your own list and start taking steps to confront these feelings without using food as a crutch.

2 **Reflect on your eating.** Take time to look back and see how far emotional eating goes. Stop blaming a certain event or situation. I did a lot of blaming when I was told to lose weight or I would lose my volleyball scholarship. I placed all my self-value in what I weighed. Up till then, I felt pretty good about who I was.

What are some possible resources that you can use to deal with your emotions? What are some healthy, constructive ways you can deal with your emotions? Do you know anyone else who has similar emotions but deals with them in a healthy way? Could that person help you? Could you follow his or her example?

3 **Look ahead.** Take time to look ahead, mapping out strategies you can use to help you deal with your emotions. I have learned to say, "I feel _____, and I can replace that feeling with _____."

You have to find your own ways of dealing with emotions. Take a negative and replace it with something positive. I found that it was like a rehearsal. I developed a list to help me when I was faced with certain emotions that popped up from time to time. Basically, this process involves learning to handle stress and to cope with problems.

When I was getting stressed out at work, I learned to share my frustrations with a coworker rather than raid the candy machine. Or I made myself go outside for a walk. My list of activities to do when I'm faced with negative emotions includes sharing, doing crafts, working on my photo album, shopping, calling friends or family, writing in a journal, reading a good play, listening to music, cleaning, and exercising. Doing something physical is a great way to get out of a bad emotional situation.

•

Start making a list of things you can do in these situations. And remember, you should eliminate eating from that list—permanently.

Success Story: Heidi

Heidi was happily married. After college, she started teaching school and fell into the couch routine, although she had always been active in sports. A typical dinner was Hamburger Helper or steak with cheesy potatoes.

"I was never skinny, but I was always active and healthy," Heidi says. Now she started to gain weight. The heavy dinners and snacking started to pile on the pounds. She was only five foot four, but she weighed 185 pounds.

Then some of the teachers at school were starting a Weight Watchers program. Heidi attended a few of the meetings and learned a lot about eating right. During the next year, she didn't stay with the program at school, but she used some of the basic information to change the way she ate, closely watching every mouthful.

"I was changing the *style* in which I ate," she says. No more meat every night, and no more cheese.

"I even changed the way I snacked," she says. "Instead of the Fritos with sour cream that I loved, I started eating healthier snacks such as pretzels."

In addition to watching what she ate, Heidi started to get more active. "I started by walking the dog every day. I felt so great after that first walk that I wanted to go out the next day and do it again. And then I was feeling so good inside and out about myself that I wanted to go farther."

Walking the dog soon led to running. "Because my dog was old, after about three miles he would get tired and just lay down," she says. "I would stand there encouraging him to keep going." Before long, she was running on her own.

In the first year of taking charge of her new healthy lifestyle, she ran her first 5K, then another and another. By 1996 Heidi had lost 40 pounds, was fit, healthy, and 145 pounds. She entered an Olympic distance triathlon in her hometown of St. Joseph, Missouri, that year and finished her first marathon in 1998.

For Heidi the change came with a commitment to watch what she eats. She just doesn't buy unhealthy foods anymore. "If they aren't there, I won't eat them," she says.

Now when she and her husband occasionally splurge on a treat such as pizza, she eats it all and that's it.

"I had a complete change in lifestyle of eating better and moving more," she says. "I have never felt so good in my life."

Once you have taken an inventory of your food habits and have kept a food diary of everything you eat (yes, everything—even those two Life Savers after lunch) for two weeks, you will have a record of your diet that you can use as a reference to apply to the following chapters on the food pyramid, portions, and nutrition. Although it may seem daunting, this process of understanding your relationship with food and your body's needs can be exhilarating. I know because that's how I feel about my own journey to maintain a healthier lifestyle.

CHAPTER 13

Size Matters: The Food Pyramid and Portions

Food, glorious food!

—*OLIVER!*, BY LIONEL BART

One of the most important lessons I've learned on my journey to health is that there's a big difference between putting food in your mouth and nourishing your body. My weight was a sign not only of poor physical fitness but also of bad eating. I stuffed myself—filling up on empty calories from soda, greasy foods, and sweet "rewards" such as cookies, doughnuts, and ice cream. I had to go back to school to learn what a portion is, how to read a label, how to shop for groceries, and how to make and eat healthy meals. Don't be ashamed of not knowing these things. I only learned about them when I asked.

Diet Is Not a Bad Word

As the years have progressed, I have learned to make healthier choices for *me*. Just because something is "healthy" doesn't mean I want to eat it. I try to follow the U.S. Department of Agriculture (USDA) food pyramid while choosing foods I enjoy.

The key is to be conscious of your diet without seeing yourself as being *on* a diet. Pay attention to the food in front of you. Try to eat sensibly and with some control. Take time to plan out good food choices that appeal to you. There are many alternatives, so you don't ever have to feel as if you are depriving yourself. Make room for the occasional sweet—it will taste even better if you make it a special treat instead of a necessity.

The Food Pyramid and What It Means to You

The food pyramid as outlined by the USDA is something I have followed to help me choose what to eat each day. Please note that this is a general guideline that can help you make easy choices based on the basic food groups.

Of course, there are other food pyramids out there, including versions for vegetarian, Mediterranean, and Asian diets. I'm not going to debate the merits of these various diets. You can make your own decisions about healthy choices. Trust me, though. There are fads popping up all the time that are just recycled diets with a new spin. If any of them really worked, we would not have any obesity in this country today. The main issues involved in our being overweight as a society (barring any medical or genetic issues) are less activity and the availability of volumes and volumes of food.

I try to make choices based on moderation and portion control, as no one food is inherently bad for you. Each of us must strike a balance between the volume of food we eat and the amount of activity we pursue. It's easy to figure out if you are out of balance. If you are gaining weight or are already overweight, you're out of balance. This usually stems from a pattern of eating too much and not moving enough—something that often happens without your even knowing it. One of my friends, Terry Martin, terms it "calories in, calories out." I was taking in lots of calories, but there was absolutely no output. So far in this book, I've discussed how to increase your output by moving more. Now it's time to talk about the second half of becoming healthy: decreasing your input.

Smart eating is essential to a healthy lifestyle. You can exercise all you want and still gain weight if you're not eating properly. Understanding the food pyramid is the first step toward eating right.

The USDA Food Guide Pyramid of daily dietary recommendations divides food into six groups. At the top of the pyramid are foods you should eat sparingly. As the pyramid gets larger toward the bottom, the suggested number of servings increases. Portion size is important in the bread, cereal, rice, and pasta group and in the fat, oils, and sweets group.

FOOD GUIDE PYRAMID
A Guide to Daily Food Choices

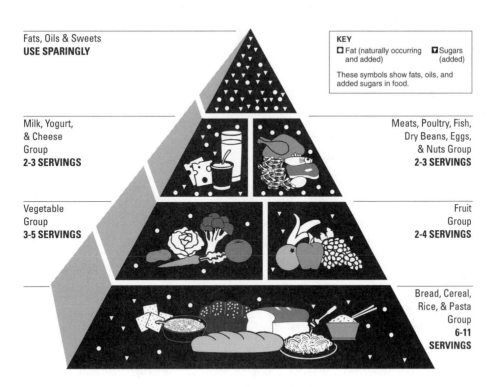

Source: U.S. Department of Agriculture and U.S. Department of Health and Human Services

That doesn't mean that as you go up the pyramid, the foods are more important. It simply means that you should eat less of those types of food each day. But keep this in mind: calories per gram of a particular food are nine calories for fat, four calories for carbohydrates, and four calories for protein. That's one reason to eat less fat.

Each of these food groups gives you some, but not all, of the nutrients you need. No one food group is more important than another. The key is to strike a balance; you need to get all of them in each day. But first you must understand what a serving size is.

I often hear comments from people who say they are exercising and eating right but can't seem to lose any weight. When I ask them how much they are eating, their problem becomes clear. I, too, had no understanding of portions in the beginning. I would down a huge plate of pasta with fat-free sauce and think I was eating well. What I didn't realize was that I was probably eating about five or six servings. Even healthy foods can put on the weight if you're not eating the right portions.

Once you have a handle on serving size, you can begin to recognize the best choices to make within the food pyramid. Let's take a look at making food choices within each group.

Bread, Cereal, Rice, and Pasta Group
6 to 11 servings
This is the group you can get into trouble with if you aren't careful about your portions. English muffins, bagels, and whole-wheat and pita bread are good choices. Also, cereals that are high in fiber and low in sugar are healthy. Try to decrease your intake of croissants, butter rolls, doughnuts, and such.

Vegetable Group
3 to 5 servings
Choose any fresh, frozen, or canned vegetable. Stay away from vegetables that are prepared in cream or butter sauces. Go for steamed or grilled instead. Remember to wash and rinse (or scrub, if appropriate) fresh vegetables before eating.

Fruit Group

2 to 4 servings

Choose any fresh, frozen, canned, or dried fruit. Stay away from canned fruits in heavy syrup, or at least rinse them off. Remember to wash and rinse (or scrub, if appropriate) fresh fruits before eating.

Milk, Yogurt, and Cheese Group

2 to 3 servings

The amount of fat in one cup of milk varies widely:

> Whole milk—8 grams of fat
>
> 2% milk—5 grams of fat
>
> 1% milk—3 grams of fat
>
> Skim milk—0 grams of fat

As for cheese, Cheddar, American, Swiss, and Monterey Jack are the highest in fat. Better choices are mozzarella or Parmesan, cottage cheese, and any cheese that is skim or low fat.

Meat, Poultry, Fish, Dry Beans, Eggs, and Nuts Group

2 to 3 servings

The best meat choices are lean beef (the tenderloin or round rump); trimmed ham; pork tenderloin; chicken or turkey without the skin; and any fish, fresh or frozen, as long as it is not breaded or fried.

You can get lots of fiber from navy beans, chickpeas, lentils, soybeans, and peanuts, and nuts such as almonds and pecans.

The guideline for eggs is no more than three yolks per week. You can eat more of the egg whites or egg substitutes.

Fats, Oils, and Sweets

Use sparingly

When using oils, go for unsaturated vegetable oils, such as olive, corn, peanut, safflower, and sesame. Watch the use of salad dressings and mayonnaise, as the calories there can add up fast.

Exercise moderation in eating sweets. Go for the low-fat or fat-free versions, but remember that these are still high in calories because there is generally a lot of sugar in them.

•

Think of the USDA food pyramid as a general guideline that can help you make choices from the basic food groups. It helped me stay with the basics but also go for variety. For example, I try to get three of my servings from the Bread, Cereal, Rice, and Pasta Group by choosing items that are also high in fiber, such as whole-wheat bread, brown rice, and high-fiber cereal. By doing this, I feel full and satisfy my daily requirements for fiber.

Take time to learn more about nutrition and eating right. Don't be lured into the latest fad diet. You didn't put on the weight overnight, and it's not going to come off overnight. Be patient and start your journey to healthy eating by becoming more conscious of what you eat. Maybe seek the advice of a registered dietitian. That old saying "You are what you eat" has been true for me: I ate high-fat foods and guess what? I got fat. Now that I've taken control of my diet, I'm at a healthier weight.

CHAPTER 14

My Shopping Cart

How do you live a long life? Take a two-mile walk every morning before breakfast.

—HARRY S. TRUMAN

My mom always told me never to go to the grocery store hungry, because you will be more likely to grab things out of impulse. Unfortunately, even if I wasn't hungry when I went grocery shopping, I knew I would be hungry soon, and going down the cookie aisle used to make my stomach growl. By the time I got to the checkout counter, my shopping cart was definitely not filled with the best choices.

I always picked up frozen dinners, frozen pizza, whole milk, orange juice, a six-pack of soda, usually two bags of cookies, a head of lettuce (which always

Drinking water is essential. Lauri Levenfeld, Zoom Photography, California

went brown before I used it), white bread, sliced meat, potato chips and dip, cheese, ice cream, Pop-Tarts, cans of soup, a box of pasta, spaghetti sauce, and a candy bar or two from the checkout aisle.

I often didn't go to the grocery store for two weeks because I ate lunch out with coworkers and headed to a fast-food restaurant for dinner. Since my schedule was so busy, I would grab what I could and wolf it down on the way to wherever I was going. Who cared about the calories or fat?

Reading Those Labels

The first step in a healthy approach to grocery shopping is knowing how to read a label. It may sound silly, but it will save you tons of calories.

This can be a bit overwhelming at first, but you don't have to be a chemist to read the nutrition fact chart that is now standard on food packaging. Once you have learned to read the chart, you can make choices quickly about the foods you are buying.

I never, ever read food labels before. I just bought what I liked and never paid attention to the contents or the serving size. Sometimes I would down a box of low-fat or fat-free cookies thinking I was at least making a healthier choice. Wrong! Quantity is important.

Also, "no fat" doesn't mean "no calorie." There can be just as many calories in a box of fat-free cookies as in a box of regular cookies, as lots of those low-fat and fat-free foods are filled with sugar. The label usually lists the nutritional values for one serving (often something silly like ten potato chips), so if you're eating more than one serving, you will have to multiply the values shown by the number of servings you're having.

Label reading is one of the best educators on nutrition. More important, when you make the commitment to be mindful of what you put into your body, you are taking a huge leap forward toward weight loss and health. On the next page are the American Heart Association's guidelines on how to read food labels.

Start looking for low-fat and fat-free products to find ones that suit your tastes. They are usually right next to the products you are already buying. For

Serving size
Is your serving the same size as the one on the label? If you eat double the serving size listed, you need to double the nutrient and calorie values. If you eat half the serving size, cut the nutrient and calorie values in half.

Calories
Are you overweight? Cut back a little on calories! Look here to see how a serving of this food adds to your daily total. A five-foot-four-inch, 138-pound active woman needs about 2,200 calories each day. A five-foot-ten-inch, 174-pound active man needs about 2,900 calories per day. Consuming more calories than your body needs will add layers of fat; consuming less (within reason), will force your body to use its stores of fat. So it pays to find out what your caloric needs are and to keep track of the calories you eat.

Total carbohydrate
When you cut down on fat, you can eat more carbohydrates. Carbohydrates are foods such as breads, potatoes, fruits, and vegetables. Choose these often. They give you more nutrients than soda and candy and more quantity for the calorie load than meat and dairy products.

Dietary fiber
Grandmother called it roughage, but her advice to eat more is still appropriate. That goes for both the soluble and insoluble kinds of dietary fiber. Fruits, vegetables, whole grain foods, beans, and peas are good sources of fiber and can help reduce the risk of heart disease and cancer.

Protein
Most Americans get more than they need. Where there is an animal protein, there is also fat and cholesterol. Eat small servings of lean meat, fish, and poultry. Use skim or low-fat milk, yogurt, and cheese. Try vegetable protein such as beans, grains, and cereals.

Vitamins and minerals
Your goal here is 100 percent of each for the day. Don't count on one food to do it all. A combination of foods adds up to a winning score.

Nutrition Facts

Serving Size ½ cup (114g)
Servings Per Container 4

Amount Per Serving

Calories 90	Calories from Fat 30
	% Daily Value*
Total Fat 3g	5%
Saturated Fat 0g	0%
Cholesterol 0mg	0%
Sodium 300mg	13%
Total Carbohydrates 13g	4%
Dietary Fiber 3g	12%
Sugars 3g	
Protein 3g	

Vitamin A	80%	●	Vitamin C	60%
Calcium	4%	●	Iron	4%

*Percent Daily Values are based on a 2,000 calorie diet. Your daily values may be higher or lower depending on your calorie needs:

	Calories	2,000	2,500
Total Fat	Less than	65g	80g
Sat Fat	Less than	20g	25g
Cholesterol	Less than	300mg	300mg
Sodium	Less than	2,400mg	2,400mg
Total Carbohydrate		300g	375g
Fiber		25g	30g

Calories per gram:
Fat 9 ● Carbohydrate 4 ● Protein 4

(More nutrients may be listed on some labels)

mg = milligrams (1,000 mg = 1 g)
g = grams (about 28 g = 1 ounce)

Source: U.S. Food and Drug Administration, provided by the American Heart Association

Total fat
Aim low. Most people need to cut back on fat. Too much fat may contribute to heart disease and cancer. Try to limit your calories from fat. For a healthy heart, choose foods with a big difference between the total number of calories and the number of calories from fat.

Saturated fat
Saturated fat is part of the total fat in food. It is listed separately because it's the key player in raising blood cholesterol and increasing your risk for heart disease. Eat less.

Cholesterol
Too much cholesterol, a second cousin to fat, can lead to heart disease. Challenge yourself to eat less than 300 mg each day.

Sodium
You call it salt, the label calls its sodium. Either way, it may add up to high blood pressure in some people. Keep your sodium intake low—2,400 to 3,000 mg or less each day. (The American Heart Association recommends no more than 3,000 mg. of sodium per day for a healthy adult.)

Daily Values
Feel like you're drowning in numbers? Let the Daily Values be your guide. Daily Values are listed for people who can eat 2,000 or 2,500 calories each day. If you eat more, your personal Daily Values may be higher than what's listed on the label. If you eat less, your personal Daily Values may be lower. For fat, saturated fat, cholesterol, and sodium, choose foods with low-percent Daily Values. For total carbohydrate, dietary fiber, and vitamins and minerals, strive for 100 percent of the Daily Values.

example, I picked up a 2.5-ounce package of ranch salad dressing and found that it had 51 grams of fat—in that little package! Reading the label helped me realize that that package of dressing didn't fit into the food pyramid recommendations or a healthy eating plan. Instead of giving up something like salad dressing entirely, I found a low-fat version of this dressing that I like.

When reading labels, I'm always aware of things I try to avoid. I want to stay as close to nature and the natural form of each food as possible. I was taught that the less a food is handled the better. For me, that meant learning to cook and forgetting about all those frozen dinners I thought were healthy.

The main things I try to avoid are artificial sweeteners such as aspartame and artificial fats such as Olestra. I also look for artificial additives such as flavors and colors when reviewing foods. I found that as I started to eliminate artificial fats and sweeteners, I acquired a new and improved taste for the natural sugars found in fruits.

It takes time to retrain your taste buds, but you can do it. I started by eliminating my daily six to eight cans of soda, even the diet brands. Water is my drink of choice. I can't believe how refreshing a piece of fruit tastes now.

With these basics in mind, you can make better choices at the grocery store. Following are some tips to remember when shopping.

Going to the Grocery Store

With a bit of planning and learning how to make healthier choices, going to the grocery store can be fun. Some of the choices you can make are as simple as finding a low-fat alternative to a high-fat food such as mayonnaise. Replace mayonnaise with mustard, or try to find a low-fat version that still has a taste you like. If you can't live without the fully loaded variety, practice moderation in how much you use.

Don't go to the grocery store when you are hungry. Otherwise, you will grab foods out of impulse. If you must shop when you are hungry, buy a piece of fresh fruit, go outside and eat it, and then commence shopping.

Also, make a grocery list. A list is a plan that will help you stay on track. I try to think of each meal as a selection of servings from the basic food groups, then plan my list around that.

Usually on the weekend, I make one trip to the grocery store to stock up for the week. If my schedule permits, I prepare a list of dinner meals and shop accordingly. I try to have a selection of foods in the house so that I can put a meal together easily when I get home.

For breakfast, I normally choose from among these options: English muffins, bagels, eggs, yogurt, oatmeal, and toast. In terms of lunch, I either brown-bag it or head to the company cafeteria. The cafeteria always has some healthy choices in the salad bar, as well as things such as turkey breast and steamed veggies.

For dinner, I always start with a long list of my favorites that I can pull together quickly. Of course, I'm always looking for new recipes. If all else fails, I usually have chicken and ground turkey on hand in the freezer. Chicken is flexible. I can combine it with pasta or grill it and serve it on a bed of lettuce with fresh vegetables. I use ground turkey to make "hamburger" patties or a rice dish.

Based on this meal plan, my shopping list usually looks something like this:

Produce	Dairy	Meat	Staples
Apples	Cottage cheese	Lean ground turkey	Bottled water
Bananas	Eggs	Skinless chicken	English muffins
Carrots	Light cheese		Fiber One cereal
Cucumbers	Skim milk		Oatmeal
Lettuce	Tofu		Pretzels
Tomatoes	Yogurt		Salsa (great on baked potatoes)
			Water-packed tuna
			Whole-wheat bread
			Whole-wheat pasta

Every few weeks, I buy staples such as pasta, peanut butter, nuts, cans of soup (such as bean or lentil), vegetarian chili, cereal, oatmeal, spices, frozen vegetables, and canned vegetables and mushrooms. These are things I know won't spoil and can be used anytime.

Going Through the Grocery Store

Stick to one or two stores so that you really get to know the layout. Avoid certain aisles, such as the cookie and snack aisles. I've found that a little planning and following a consistent route around the store saves time and helps me make healthy choices.

Produce

In most stores, the produce section is in the front as you walk in. This is the one area of the store where I urge you to go a little crazy. Here you have endless choices of foods packed with vitamins and healthy benefits. These foods will help you get the two to four servings of fruits and three to five servings of vegetables each day that the USDA food pyramid suggests.

Here is just a partial list of my produce basics. I urge you to try fruits and vegetables that you've never had before. You might find something you like. Try to buy in batches—four pieces of three kinds—so that you'll have enough around for snacks.

Fruits		**Vegetables**	
Apples	Plums	Beets	Mushrooms
Bananas	Raspberries	Boston lettuce	Onions
Blueberries	Strawberries	Broccoli	Radishes
Cantaloupe	Tangerines	Broccoli rabe	Red peppers
Grapefruit	Watermelon	Carrots	Romaine lettuce
Grapes		Cauliflower	Spinach
Honeydew melon		Celery	Sugar snap peas
Kiwifruit		Collard greens	Tomatoes
Mangoes		Corn	
Oranges		Cucumbers	
Papayas		Green beans	
Peaches		Green peppers	
Pears		Mesclun	

As you come out of the produce section, sometimes you are faced with the bakery. Keep pushing your cart past here unless you are looking for fresh bread.

Deli

Use caution here; many of those salads are high in fat due to the use of mayonnaise. Make sure to ask how the salads are prepared. By contrast, you can find low-fat turkey and chicken breast for sandwiches here.

Fresh Fish and Meat

Depending on the store, you will find a variety of fish in this section. If you are looking for meat, go for the lean cuts. Instead of ground beef, look for ground turkey or chicken. When choosing chicken pieces, try to select skinless cuts. And for faster cooking, go for skinless boneless cuts.

Bread

For the healthiest choice, stick with whole-wheat or multigrain bread. But make sure that whole-grain flour is the first ingredient. If wheat flour or unbleached wheat flour comes first, the bread is made mainly of refined flour, which is not as good for you. Don't buy white bread; it's just empty carbohydrate calories. But just because a bread is dark doesn't mean it's whole grain. Some dark breads may appear to be healthier, but if they're made with molasses or brown sugar, they're actually less healthy.

Rice crackers are a great alternative to bread. Choose the plain ones, not the ones that are flavored with sugar or cheese.

Chips

The fat adds up fast in this aisle, but making a choice such as baked over fried chips can save you up to 50 percent of the fat per serving. But don't buy fat-free chips that are made with artificial fats such as Olestra. They may seem healthier, but they're not, because they have synthetic ingredients, which are not good for you.

Tortilla chips can have as much fat as potato chips, so look for low-fat or baked chips instead. Choose pretzels over potato chips or corn chips. Pretzels have no fat and are a great snack compared to the other options in this aisle. (Remember, they do have salt.)

You'll also find microwave popcorn and traditional popcorn in this aisle. Air-popped corn is always the healthiest choice, but many microwave brands are low fat or fat-free. Just remember to read the labels.

Soda

When you drink regular soda, you are taking in hundreds of empty calories of sugar. Even diet soda contains artificial sweeteners, which are not healthy. Try to abstain from all soda.

As an alternative, check out the bottled water section, usually at the end of this aisle or one aisle over. You can jazz up your water by purchasing flavored seltzer or adding fresh lemon, lime, or orange slices to plain water.

Frozen Food

Consider giving vegetable patties a try. They are low in fat and sometimes taste better than most beef burgers. Another great option is perogies, a type of pasta filled with potatoes that makes a great side dish or low-fat meal in itself (just add some vegetables). Look for recipes on the package.

Watch out for frozen dinners. I picked up a box of chicken recently, and the label reported 22 grams of fat per piece. Chicken is healthy, but not this chicken! Aim for low-fat frozen entrées, but beware: just because they seem to be healthy doesn't mean that they are.

Another option is frozen pasta or veggies with sauce that you just have to add meat to. Make sure that the sauce doesn't have too much fat, however.

Generally stay away from ice cream and frozen treats. They are just empty calories. But if you must indulge, avoid high-fat ice cream. Instead, choose a low-fat option with a taste you enjoy. Sorbet and frozen yogurt can be great-tasting, healthier alternatives. You may have to experiment with several brands to find one that is right for you.

Sandwich Meat

Here you can find numerous choices for sandwich meats, bacon, sausage, and hot dogs. Really be aware of the fat content of these items. For example, look at this breakdown of common sandwich meats:

Bologna	13	grams of fat
Ham	3.3	grams of fat
Salami	18	grams of fat
Turkey	5	grams of fat

And that is usually for only two or three slices of meat. Read the labels, as manufacturers are offering some lower-fat versions of all sandwich meats. Also watch for salt content.

In terms of bacon and sausage, all I can say is they have a lot of fat for a small portion. If you really want these items, make sure you have a small amount and not every day. Also look at the new options for turkey sausage and bacon, as well as vegetarian versions, which are pretty good.

Hot dogs have 15 grams of fat each, so limit your intake and look for turkey or vegetarian dogs instead.

Juice and Dairy Products

You have all kinds of options for juices. There are even lots of options just for orange juice—with added calcium, with or without pulp, and so on.

Juice is not a bad item. There is sugar in it, though, so don't drink juice instead of water, and don't drink too much each day. Generally, one or two glasses are all you need. Sometimes it's better to go for the whole orange instead of just the juice.

In this section, you will also find eggs, which are a great source of protein. Limit your intake to a few eggs each week as part of your daily meals.

Cheese is good for you, but you can really bulk up on fat by eating too much. Try the lower-fat or fat-free versions. You may have to experiment to get a good-tasting alternative. For example, if you want cream cheese, you can choose from these options (fat and calories per one tablespoon):

Regular	4.8 grams of fat	50 calories
Light	2.5 grams of fat	31 calories
Low fat or fat-free	0.7 grams of fat	18 calories

Choosing a lower-fat alternative can make a big difference in your diet.

You'll also find milk in this section. You may also consider trying soy or rice milk, which offers many health benefits and isn't high in fat.

Look for low-fat or fat-free yogurt here. You'll find many options to choose from.

There's a big debate about whether you should eat butter or margarine. Butter is not bad in moderation. Margarine is a hydrogenated fat, which means that the chemical makeup of the fat is changed in the processing, and it may not have any advantage over butter. In my opinion, butter is better, but use it sparingly, as the USDA food pyramid advises.

Peanut Butter and Jelly

Peanut butter can be a good source of protein, but it is high in fat. Eating it in moderation, or even switching to a lower-fat version, is okay. It can be a nice addition to your breakfast toast. But read those labels, as peanut butter can have 16 or more grams of fat per two tablespoons.

Jelly has no fat but as much as 50 calories per tablespoon. Look for light versions that are sugar-free. When used in moderation, it's fine, especially as a substitute for butter on toast.

Also in this aisle, you'll find gelatin and pudding. Gelatin has no fat and is low in calories. Sugar-free versions are also available. This can be a nice snack if you throw in some fruit as well.

Honey is often in the same aisle. Although honey has no fat, it does have calories. If used in moderation, though, it can be a good sweetener.

Baking Goods

Sure, all the cookie and cake mixes are in this aisle, but it also has a great selection of herbs and spices to jazz up your food. Also look for premixed packages of seasonings to add to your meat, chicken, fish, or stir-fry dishes.

Cereal

Here you have a chance to make several good choices. But you need to read the labels for sugar and fat content. You might think that granola is healthy, but one brand I used to eat had 22 grams of fat per serving. Stay away from sugary cereals and stick to high-fiber, whole grain cereals.

Oatmeal is a great low-fat breakfast item. Top it off with some fresh fruit to start your day off right.

Beware of the granola and breakfast bars in this aisle. They can be a quick snack, but they may be high in fat and sugar.

Also in this aisle are pancake mixes and syrup. If you love pancakes, check out some of the low-fat mixes. Also try some of the sugar-free syrup alternatives.

Rice and Pasta

White rice and whole-grain brown rice both have around 165 calories and less than 1 gram of fat per serving. But it is better to stick to brown rice because it is more nutritious.

There are many shapes and sizes of pasta, which is a great source of carbohydrates and can be a meal or a side dish. The problem I have with pasta is that I eat too much. Did you know that one serving of pasta is only one-half cup? So enjoy pasta—maybe even consider whole-wheat pasta—but watch your portions.

Pasta sauces also come in numerous variations. Just take time to check out the fat content before making your selection. If a sauce has meat or cheese in it, the fat content will be higher. Some sauces that you think are healthy have hidden fat because of the oil in them. Try to stick to basic sauces that are made with tomatoes and vegetables.

Also in this aisle are many "meal-in-a-box" items such as Hamburger Helper and macaroni and cheese. You really have to read the labels here because those sauces can add up to a lot of fat and calories.

Finally, you will find canned beans—navy, kidney, lima, and black beans—in this aisle. These are awesome to cook with and are very healthy.

Canned Soup, Tuna, and Vegetables

Stay away from cream-based soups, as they are often high in fat. Many soup brands offer low-salt versions. Make sure to read the labels.

Tuna is a great choice for a healthy meal, but stick with water-packed tuna. Beware of premixed tuna salad, which is often high in fat due to the mayonnaise.

Canned veggies are a staple for the cupboard. Pick up your favorites to have on hand so that you can create instant side dishes. Choose ones that are packed in water with no sugar added. Low-salt varieties also are available.

Cookies and Crackers

Avoid this aisle if you can. Even low-fat and fat-free cookies have a lot of sugar and, therefore, a lot of calories. If you need to have cookies, eat them in moderation or try to substitute graham crackers.

As for crackers, make sure you check out the labels. Some crackers can have as much 1 gram of fat per cracker. Baked versions are a better alternative.

Salad Dressing and Condiments

A salad dressing can change a healthy salad into a fat disaster if you don't pay attention to the label. Here are some examples (fat and calories per one tablespoon):

Blue cheese	7.5 grams of fat	75 calories
French	5.3 grams of fat	53 calories
Italian	5 grams of fat	50 calories
Ranch	7.1 grams of fat	68 calories
Thousand Island	5 grams of fat	55 calories

Taste is an issue here, but many of the low-fat and fat-free versions are good-tasting. Also remember portion size. When was the last time you put only a tablespoon of dressing on your salad?

The condiments in this aisle include mayonnaise, ketchup, mustard, and tartar sauce. Start reading those labels for the healthy differences you can make with some small changes.

Mayonnaise can add a lot of fat and calories to a sandwich: 10.9 grams of fat and 94 calories per tablespoon. Look for a lighter version that has only 2.9 grams of fat and 35 calories per tablespoon.

Ketchup is fat-free and has as few as 15 calories per tablespoon.

Mustard also is a low-fat, low-calorie condiment. Make sure to read the labels, though, because some mustards contain fat.

Tartar sauce has 18.4 grams of fat and 170 calories in two tablespoons. Imagine how fast a nice grilled or baked fish can turn into a high-fat disaster.

Other condiments in this aisle have little or no fat and few calories but can add great flavor to a meal. Here are some options:

Barbecue sauce

Chili sauce

Cocktail sauce

Hot sauce

Salsa

Tabasco

Salsa is a great choice, as it has only 10 to 15 calories per tablespoon and no fat.

You'll also find pickles and oils in this aisle. Pickles have no fat and are low in calories. As for oils, make sure to use virgin olive, sunflower, canola, or safflower oil instead of corn oil. Also consider using vegetable cooking spray, which is fat-free.

CHAPTER 15

One Bite at a Time: Nutrition and Eating Basics That Can Work for You

We have obtained this life as a human being. Whether we make it worthwhile or not depends on our mental attitude.

—THE DALAI LAMA

Once I had established which foods are healthy and which aren't, I had to learn how to eat them. This was the trickiest part for me—the most emotional, challenging, and, ultimately, rewarding experience.

How can you make the miracle of transformation happen? Take it one bite at a time. Make conscious choices about what you will eat and when you will eat. Ask yourself why you are eating. You're probably making most of your choices out of habit. That's why it's such a shock to keep a food journal and see what you've actually been eating without even noticing. Habits can change. Change begins with a thought, the thought leads to an action, the action leads to a habit, and habits lead to character, or who you really are. It starts so simply: think before you eat.

You Must Eat

The first thing everyone has to learn about nutrition is this: you must eat. No matter what you weigh, you need to feed your body to get healthy—particularly if you want to lose weight. I've tried some diets where I was actually starving myself—eating almost nothing—and although I lost a few pounds, I felt horrible and gained the weight back as soon as I started eating again. My nutritionist, Evelyn Cole-Kissinger, taught me that when you starve the body, it slows down your metabolism and starts hoarding the calories you do eat. Skipping breakfast and eating five doughnuts a day wasn't helping me. It was hurting my body, depriving it of what it needed to work properly, and thus keeping me in a constant state of craving those high-fat, sugary foods that would give me a quick burst of energy. Then I'd crash twenty minutes after eating one, and the craving would begin all over again. It was a relief to start thinking about food as something that fuels your body. Good food—the kinds of food we discussed in Chapter 14—is good for you.

What's Healthy for You?

You need to personalize the eating program that works for you. Each of us is different. Read through the following suggestions, and decide which ones fit you and your lifestyle. I can tell you, a nutritionist can tell you, and your mother can tell you that tofu is good for you. But if you can't gag it down, it's not going to help you at all. Now take a look at your food lifestyle. Remember, be honest.

- What emotions trigger your overeating episodes?
- What can you do to handle your emotions instead of eating?
- How can you space your meals to keep you from becoming overly hungry?
- What foods do you like and dislike?
- Can you eat at home most of the time, or does your job and life demand that you eat on the go?
- How do you get yourself up in the morning?
- Do you drink lots of coffee?

- Do you eat sugary foods in the morning to boost your energy?
- Do you eat breakfast at home?
- Could you eat breakfast at home?
- Do you eat a late-morning snack?
- Do you eat lunch out every day?
- Can you find healthy foods to eat near your work?
- Can you pack a lunch of whole-wheat bread and a couple of fruits?
- What do you eat for a snack in the afternoon?
- Can you keep fruit at your desk at work or in your kitchen at home as an alternative to cookies, candy, ice cream, and the like?
- What do you usually eat for dinner?
- What would you like to eat for dinner?
- Do you eat while watching TV?
- Do you eat dinner in less than twenty minutes?
- What is your ideal meal?
- What is a healthy meal?
- Do you drink water?

With the answers to these questions, you'll be on the road to understanding your eating habits and creating your own personal eating program—a healthy program that works for you.

Evelyn's Guidelines

Here are some guidelines and suggestions that Evelyn gave me to jump-start my thinking about making better and healthier food choices.

1 **Fuel your body.** You need to eat to reach and maintain your healthy weight. You need to eat more filling foods—foods that really satisfy you, foods that give you energy, foods that make you feel good, whole foods, plant-based foods, high-fiber foods, complex carbohydrate foods. It may not be the amount of food you are eating that is causing your health challenge. It may be the kinds of food you are eating, when you are eating them, and why you are eating them. When you eat more wholesome foods, you will experience greater success in getting control of your weight and well-being.

2 **Write down what you eat.** Write down the time you eat, the food(s) eaten, any beverages you drink, and approximately how much you consume. You may want to record any triggers you're aware of that make you want eat. See if any emotional issues are leading you to food. You also may want to record fiber or fats to help you learn about foods. Your food record can help you see your progress and how to make better choices tomorrow. If you find that you get hungry at 10:30 A.M., you probably need to eat a higher-fiber breakfast. If you need a snack at 3:30 P.M., you probably need a higher-fiber lunch.

3 **Eat meals at regular times.** Once you know, through your food diary, when you're hungriest, you can schedule your meals around those times. When you're not constantly staving off hunger, you'll be more successful at reaching and maintaining a healthy weight. When you have a controlled appetite, it's easier to make healthy food choices. When you eat is important. Space meals about four to six hours apart.

4 **Drink water.** Sometimes just developing one new habit can make a big difference. For instance, take a bottle of water with you wherever you go. Buy water instead of soda when you go to the convenience store. Having water handy makes it easier to drink when you're thirsty. You may even find yourself reaching for your water bottle instead of a snack.

Do you ever confuse the hunger signal for the thirst signal? Next time you feel hungry, drink a glass or two of water and see if that satisfies you. Your body is probably craving water and you don't even know it.

Thirst is not a reliable indicator of your water needs. When you get used to drinking water, you will begin to get thirsty. Drink at least six to eight glasses (eight ounces each) of water each day. It's quite easy to do once you get in the habit. Drink a couple of glasses of water when you first get up. Drink two glasses between breakfast and lunch. Drink two glasses between lunch and supper.

Choose water at mealtimes instead of other beverages. When you get used to water, you will prefer it to high-calorie, high-sugar, caffeinated drinks. How many calories would you save if your beverage of choice was water?

5 **Eat more fiber.** High-fiber foods will help you reach and maintain your healthy weight. These foods are low in calories and high in bulk. Your appetite will be satisfied from one meal to the next without the need for between-meal snacks.

Fiber foods will satisfy your appetite and reduce your cravings for sugar, chocolate, and snacks. You may crave sugar because your body needs energy, because your serotonin level is low, or because you're just in the habit of eating sugar. Fiber foods will boost your energy level and provide lasting energy. Just ask an athlete about complex carbohydrates (fiber foods). He or she will tell you that these are the best energy foods. Fiber foods also raise your serotonin level. And fiber foods keep your blood sugar level more stable. When your blood sugar is low, you may crave a snack. You'll be amazed at the control you feel when you concentrate on eating fiber foods.

Fiber foods also build a healthy body. They are rich in vitamins, minerals, antioxidants, and phytochemicals. This army of nutrients protects your cells. If a cell is damaged, these nutrients appear to repair and rebuild it. Fiber foods offer protection from heart disease, cancer, hypertension, diabetes, hypoglycemia, pre-menstrual syndrome (PMS), menopause complications, constipation, colon diseases, and aging. With a list like that, you can't afford not to take advantage of these great foods.

What are fiber foods? Fiber foods are foods that grow in nature: vegetables, fruits, beans, and whole grains. It's as simple as that: eat foods as they are grown. Eat fresh vegetables and fruits. Have beans more often. Eat whole-grain breads. Eat whole-grain cereals.

When you get full on fiber foods, you won't crave so many less healthy foods. Think positive. Ask yourself, "What can I eat that's high in fiber?" or "What am I eating that has fiber?" Instead of thinking, "I can have this or that," think "I can eat until I'm satisfied when I eat fiber foods."

How much fiber is enough? The recommendation for dietary fiber is 30 to 50 grams a day. Most Americans get about 6 to 10 grams of fiber a day. You can easily increase the amount of fiber you get by eating more vegetables and fruits, whole-grain breads and cereals, and beans. They are the highest-fiber foods. In one cup of beans, you get 18 grams of fiber—half of what you need for the day. A one-cup serving of a fruit or vegetable contains 6 to 10 grams of fiber.

Read the labels to find out how much dietary fiber is in packaged foods. When you choose bread, choose one that has at least 2 grams of fiber per slice. When you choose cereal, choose one with at least 3 to 5 grams of fiber—the more fiber, the better. A better choice is a whole-grain cooked cereal such as oatmeal or a seven-grain cereal such as Red River.

6 **Eat less fat.** Fats are loaded with calories—twice the calories of protein or carbohydrates. Try to limit your fat intake to around 30 grams for women and 40 grams for men per day. One teaspoon of margarine, butter, or oil has about 5 grams of fat. Do you really need those two big globs of butter on your toast or potato? Could you be happy with less?

Consider your serving size of meat. Each ounce of high-fat meat has 8 grams of fat, so an eight-ounce steak has 64 grams of fat. Instead of high-fat meats, fill your plate with high-fiber, low-calorie vegetables, and whole grains. When having meat, choose chicken, turkey, or fish.

You need to look at the number of fat grams as well as the total fat. How many fat grams are there in a serving of chips? How much is a serving? How many servings in a bag? How much of that bag did you eat? Read the labels.

7 **Eat less sugar.** Eating high-fiber foods usually curbs the sugar monster. But sugar creates an appetite for itself. The more you eat, the more you want. If you still struggle with sugar even when you're eating high-fiber foods, you may want to make a conscious effort to reduce your sugar intake. Pay attention to when you get sugar cravings. Are they related to low energy, emotions, or stress? When you get the urge to snack, stop, listen to your body, and ask yourself these questions.

Make a conscious effort to reduce your sugar intake for one week. After a week, your taste buds will adjust and probably be happier with less sugar. A reasonable intake of sugar is about 30 to 40 grams per day. Every 4 grams you read on the label tells you that there is one teaspoon of sugar in the product. Eight to ten teaspoons of sugar a day is within reason. Of course, the less refined sugar you eat, the better.

Do not include the sugar found naturally in fruits and milk in your count. There are about 10 to 15 grams of natural sugar in fruits and about 12 grams in one cup of milk. One place you may be getting a lot of sugar is in soda. Many twelve-ounce cans of soda have 30 to 40 grams of sugar. Give your body a break; drink water instead of soda.

Some people are very sensitive to added sugar and feel that if they eat any added sugar, they'll go into a sugar binge. Observe your behavior and see if added sugar is a controllable substance for you.

8 **Eat breakfast.** To reach and maintain your healthy weight and to enjoy vibrant health, eat breakfast. The more breakfast, the better. Eat a large bowl of cereal, a piece or two of toast, and a couple of fruits. You'll be amazed at how controlled your appetite will be for the rest of the day. Don't worry about the calories in your breakfast when they come from fiber foods. You have time to use them all up. Your metabolism is higher in the early part of the day, and you will burn calories better. Try to eat breakfast within two hours after you get up. If you're pressed for time or don't like breakfast foods, eat a sandwich or two and a fruit on the way to work. You may even like the leftovers from supper for breakfast.

Eat breakfast even if you're not hungry. You're probably not hungry because you're still full from supper and snacks the night before. If you're skipping breakfast, I bet you're having trouble with overeating in the evenings. Often Chub Club members say to me, "I do well all day, but by five P.M. I'm starving. I eat supper, but I'm not full, so I keep on eating until I go to bed." Stop the cycle. Get up in the morning and eat as much breakfast as you can. Eating a healthy, high-fiber breakfast provides relief from most snack attacks—even evening snacks. Start your day off right with a full stomach.

9 **Eat more fiber at lunch.** If you have been eating burgers and fries, you're in for a treat when you decide to choose a high-fiber lunch. You know how you get hungry a couple of hours after downing a meal? Well, with a high-fiber lunch, you'll be satisfied for hours. None of those cravings for candy bars and soda. You'll feel satisfied. Choose a sandwich or two on whole-wheat bread, some fresh veggies, and a couple of fruits. Delicious!

Eat lunch even if you're not hungry. If you skip lunch, you'll get overly hungry and find yourself tired, cranky, and susceptible to high-fat, sugary foods later in the day. Keep your appetite under control by eating a high-fiber lunch. Think about taking your lunch with you. If you go out to eat, go to places that serve sandwiches on whole-grain bread. Take along an apple or another fruit to eat on the way to lunch or after lunch.

10 **Eat dinner at least four hours before you go to bed.** You'll have a more restful sleep. Be sure to eat plenty of high-fiber vegetables at dinner. If you need an evening snack, eat fresh fruit, fresh veggies, or a bowl of high-fiber cereal.

Healthy Eating *Is* Healthy Eating

These ten suggestions should get you started thinking about how and why you eat and what changes will help you achieve a healthier lifestyle. I have found over the years that healthy eating *is* healthy eating. When I started making better food choices, I started to like those foods and they became a pleasurable part of my day. I was so surprised at how my taste buds changed. This didn't happen overnight. I was patient with the progress I made and focused on the long term. I wanted to make good health a part of my life, not a quick fix to be discarded as soon as possible.

You'll benefit, too, from making healthier food choices. It may be hard to believe, but in time you will actually prefer a healthy snack to a high-sugar, high-fat snack. You'll prefer baked over fried. And you'll love how you feel when you eat a hearty breakfast.

As I paid attention to my eating choices, my body became healthier on the inside and out. When you are healthier physically, you are healthier mentally and spiritually. Those things all work together.

When you choose healthy food, you're literally choosing life. You will feel better, look better, have better lab values (glucose, blood cholesterol, triglycerides, and so on), even get along better with others. Your outlook and your relationships will change. Start eating healthy with a view toward renewing your life and yourself. Stop using food as a crutch. If you believe you can get healthy, you can. If you want to do it, you will.

Tricks of the Trade

Evelyn's ten suggestions are the key to healthy eating, but here are some other tricks that I've learned from Chub Club members, websites, nutritionists, trainers, and friends that have helped supplement them:

- A two-ounce packet of ranch dressing has 230 calories and 21 grams of fat. Eliminate that and you're halfway home for the day. A lighter dressing could mean 50 calories and 0 fat. A squeeze of lemon and some freshly ground pepper tastes great on salad greens—and you're adding no fat and no calories.
- Mayonnaise has 10 to 15 grams of fat per tablespoon. If you can't bear to eliminate mayonnaise entirely, try a light version that has half the calories. Or use ketchup or mustard. Mustard has no calories and no fat. Ketchup has 15 calories per tablespoon.
- Barbecue sauce has a lot more flavor than mustard or ketchup. With a little searching, you should be able to find one that tastes good and has only 40 calories per tablespoon and no fat.

- Salsa, with 10 calories per tablespoon and no fat, is great on a baked potato instead of sour cream.
- Sauerkraut is another great alternative to sour cream.
- A Big Mac has 31 grams of fat and 560 calories. Large fries? 450 calories and 22 grams of fat. Put your fast-food favorites on your "special treats" list and take them off your diet staples list.
- A twelve-ounce can of soda has the equivalent of twelve teaspoons of sugar. Diet sodas containing various forms of low-cal sweeteners have actually been shown to make you hungry. Water has no fat and no calories—and your body needs it. If you don't like the taste, use bottled instead of tap water. If you still don't like it, try a little squeeze of fresh lemon or lime, add some ice on a hot day, and it's wonderful!
- If you're trying to cut down on salt, use freshly ground pepper. It enhances the flavor of food in much the same way that salt does, and tastes much, much better than store-bought ground pepper. Just watch the Food Network sometime—those famous chefs put freshly ground pepper in *everything*!
- Before a workout, try a can of Ensure Light. It has 200 calories and will give you enough energy to get through any workout.
- A high-fiber diet fills you up fast. Consider a cereal that has a high fiber content, such as Fiber One.
- Looking for a fun treat? Dip your apple in fat-free caramel.
- Another great treat is a piece of celery with peanut butter on it.
- Stay away from enriched flour.
- After you eat, immediately go and brush your teeth. You really don't want to eat or drink anything after brushing your teeth.
- The later you eat, the longer food sits in your stomach. You don't sleep well, you end up tired, and your body is fatigued because it has been working on digestion.
- The biggest meal of the day should be lunch, and then breakfast. Dinner should be light.
- The first year after my visit to the doctor's office, I decided to follow a vege-

tarian lifestyle. Because of that, I couldn't eat at McDonald's or Wendy's. It kept me out of the fast-food restaurants.

- Subway is a great fast-food alternative. A lot of their sandwiches are under 300 calories. Their six-inch vegetarian sandwich on whole wheat has 3 grams of fat and 222 calories.
- Always opt for whole-wheat bread, and avoid the fast-food chicken and turkey sandwiches like the plague.
- One Chub Clubber told me that as soon as she gets her dinner at a restaurant she has the waiter bring a box and put half the dinner in it. She eats it for lunch the next day. My mother does that now.
- Smaller meals are better. Now I can't eat a really big meal—I eat smaller meals more frequently.
- One Chub Clubber eats with a baby spoon and a baby fork because it slows her down.
- Another trick is to use smaller bowls and plates, which makes the portions look bigger.
- Believe it or not, the color of the tablecloth is important. Red is not good, because red stimulates you, so you eat more.

Your Tastes Will Change

Not long ago, I went jogging with my boyfriend, Rick. It was cold and rainy, and we decided to turn around. We cut down this side street and went by "fast-food row." I could smell the fat from the doughnut shop, and I almost threw up. I used to *love* doughnuts.

Everyone wants to hear that I found some miracle diet, some weight-loss secret. They don't want to hear about the food pyramid, about changing their lifestyle, about learning what a portion is, about reading labels. Diets are sexier. But they *don't work.*

I try to keep current and stick to reliable sources, like the American Medical Association and the American Dietetic Association. But people think that's boring. They want to hear about Sugar Busters, the Blood Type Diet, the Zone Diet.

I used to eat my last meal at 9:30 or 10:00 P.M. Now I try to eat dinner before 7:00 P.M. You should eat at least three hours and preferably four hours before going to bed.

I was always eating on the run. I never paid attention when I was eating. I learned to take twenty minutes or so to eat and stay focused on what I was doing for that whole time. The nutritionist taught me to put my fork down between bites and concentrate on chewing. If you eat really fast, sometimes you don't register that you ate. Since dining gives emotional as well as physical satisfaction, you end up hungry for more. The key to eating well is to *slow down*.

I started reading every label and eventually eliminated processed food and frozen dinners from my diet. You're better off eating the box.

CHAPTER 16

Ask Judy: Frequently Asked Chub Club Questions

JUST FOR TODAY

Just for today, I will live through the next 12 hours and not tackle my whole life's problems at once.

Just for today, I will improve my mind, learn something useful. Read something that requires effort, thought and concentration.

Just for today, I will be agreeable, look my best, speak in a well-modulated voice . . . be courteous and considerate.

Just for today, I will not find fault with friends, relatives or colleagues. I will not try to change or improve anyone but myself.

I will have a program. I might not follow it exactly, but I will have it. Two enemies, "hurry" and "indecision," I will not have.

I will do a good turn and keep it secret. I will do things just for exercise.

I will be unafraid and enjoy beauty.

As I give to the world . . . the world will give to me.

—ANONYMOUS

As coach of the Chub Club, I hear a lot of questions from people all over the country who are just like I was—starving for information, eager to get healthy, needing a little help to get started. I learned a lot over the years by doing, reading, and researching. I'm studying for my certification in personal training and health weight management consulting. Here are some of the most common questions I receive, along with my best advice.

I'm smiling here because I made it through 54-degree water during the Escape from Alcatraz Triathlon!

When I am traveling, how can I eat right and exercise?

Traveling for business or vacation can put a bump in the road of your routine. When I travel for business:

- I always make sure to book a hotel that has a fitness area and/or a pool.
- I always carry a bottle of water and my own healthy snacks, particularly when traveling by plane.
- If the flight is a long one, I always call twenty-four hours ahead and request a special meal or a fruit plate.
- I try to walk everywhere. (Some hotels have jogging paths and maps of nearby places where you can walk or run. You do need to be careful about safety, however.)
- I use the hotel as a workout maze. I go up and down the stairs several times. I do push-ups, sit-ups, chair dips, stretching, and basic calisthenics right in my room.
- I pack resistance bands and even a couple of small dumbbells for a strength workout in my room.

The key is to plan ahead and use whatever is at hand. For instance, find a video or a book to teach you some simple exercises that you can do anytime and anywhere.

Will lifting weights make me big and bulky?

No, unless you plan on spending hours and hours training to be a body-builder. Try to think of lifting weights as strength training. You are doing so much good for your bones and body when you add strength training to your cardio routine. It's the best way to reshape your body, tone your muscles, and increase your metabolism.

To start a routine that involves strength training, look for a certified personal trainer. Many gyms and health clubs offer these services as part of their programs. If you'd rather work out at home, or if your local health clubs don't offer personal trainers, look in the Yellow Pages for a trainer who takes private clients. Meet with the trainer, discuss your goals, and have him or her set up a routine for you.

Make sure your trainer is someone you trust and someone who can motivate you. Your trainer will not only show you what to do and how many repetitions of each exercise to do, but he or she also will show you how to do each exercise the right way. A sit-up done wrong will strain your back and do nothing for your stomach. Weight work and circuit training (a fancy word for a series of exercises) done properly can have dramatic results.

You can also check out videos and books on the subject to learn the proper techniques to avoid injury. Ask a family member to watch (or spot) you, give you feedback, and make sure you're safe. Use a mirror to be sure you're in the right position (you're not arching your back or locking up your joints).

How do I get rid of flabby arms?

Rudely known as bingo arms, they flap and wave as you walk, and you get rid of them with strength work. Spot reducing works best. Complement this with a consistent cardio routine and a healthy diet. You can add strength training to your routine slowly, starting with dumbbell exercises for the triceps area. Dips using a bench or

Me and my dad at my first Ironman.

chair for support can really help tone that area. But don't stop there. Keep adding strength-training exercises for overall toning and muscular fitness.

What can I do for exercise when pregnant?

You definitely need to speak with your obstetrician about your current health and fitness level and the exercise guidelines for you to follow while pregnant. There are many great benefits to exercising while pregnant, but you need to know your limits. Your doctor is likely to tell you it's okay to keep doing any type of exercise you were doing regularly before you got pregnant. In general, this is not a good time to start anything new—except walking.

Look for a video of exercise routines you can do while pregnant. Many health clubs and hospitals also offer exercise classes for pregnant women. Again, check with your doctor first.

I have bad knees and can't run. What can I do?

With bad knees, you must be careful about the type of impact exercises you do, as they can put additional strain on your joints. Talk with your doctor about any limitations you might have. Many people with knee problems find swimming, deep-water running, and water aerobics a good way to keep moving without putting any stress on your knees.

How can I find out what my ideal weight is?

There are many charts out there that explain what your ideal weight should be, but they don't seem to agree. Currently, the most common chart being used is the Body Mass Index (BMI) to determine whether you are overweight or obese. I have concerns about this index because it doesn't take all the relevant factors into consideration—elite athletes and very fit people are often considered overweight by the chart guidelines because of their muscle mass.

Any guideline for weight has to be just that—a guideline. It may be helpful to use a range for your ideal weight. Other indicators, such as body fat percentage and lab values (cholesterol, triglycerides, and so on), may be better indicators of health.

How much weight is safe to lose each week?

The recommended safe and maintainable weight loss is one pound a week.

How much water should I drink each day?

It is recommended that you drink at least eight glasses (eight ounces each) of water each day. If you are exercising, you will need to increase that amount. I usually carry a bottle of water with me everywhere I go so I am never without it. Also, when you are exercising, get into the habit of drinking four to six ounces of water every fifteen to twenty minutes.

If you're exercising outdoors, that means taking water with you. There are many water systems that let you carry a water bottle or two on your bike. Backpack-style bottles, or camelbacks, hold a lot of water and are very useful when you're going to be gone for more than an hour. Most come with a tube that lets you take a sip without using your hands. When running, I use a system called a Fuel Belt that wraps around my waist.

How long before exercising should I eat?

That depends on the type of workout you're going to do and your stomach. But you don't want to eat too much before exercising, as it can cause stomach cramps and nausea—and even an unexpected trip to the bathroom.

I was taught that you should allow two to three hours after a small meal and three to four hours after a big meal. But if you are rushing off to a workout, it helps to eat a snack that is high in carbohydrates and easy to digest, so that you have that extra push of energy to get you through. I often go for a bagel, an energy sports bars (keep trying, and you'll find one you like), bananas, or a liquid nutritional drink such as Ensure Light. Drink a couple of glasses of water about a half hour before you exercise to help keep you from getting dehydrated.

Another trick I discovered during races is to avoid high-fat and high-fiber foods before a workout. Again, you may need to make a run for the bathroom.

How do I kick the soda routine?

The best way is by doing it slowly and cutting back a little each day. When I gave up soda, I had a massive headache for a few weeks. I was going through a major caffeine withdrawal.

Another good reason to give up sugary sodas is the number of empty calories in each can. Sure, you can switch to diet versions, but then you are confronted with artificial sweeteners and extra salt. Research on diet soda shows that it can affect your metabolism. In fact, it may be even worse for you than regular soda.

When reaching for a soda, substitute a glass of water with a slice of lemon or lime. If you love those little bubbles, try seltzer. Be cautious about drinking too much juice, though, because it contains a lot of sugar.

How much protein do you need each day?

The amount of protein you need is based on your weight and your activity level. Here's the formula my nutritionist gave me: 0.8 grams of protein per kilogram (2.2 pounds) of body weight (a bit more if you are active). Getting enough protein in your diet isn't difficult, as most Americans' diets contain too much protein. Try to eat some protein with each meal, though.

Are carbohydrates bad for me?

Carbohydrates are getting a bad rap. Several popular diets advise eliminating carbohydrates or reducing your intake dramatically. The USDA recommended guideline for carbohydrates in a healthy diet is 50 to 60 percent of your daily intake. Carbohydrates in themselves are not bad for you, but beware of the amount you eat. It all comes down to "calories in, calories out." The source of your calories isn't as important as the quantity. Carbohydrates burn quickly when you are active.

When I am not eating enough carbohydrates, my exercise sessions suffer. I try to stick to whole foods—fruits, vegetables, and whole grains—instead of bread and pasta.

How can I get energy from what I eat?

I remember a filmstrip in school that compared eating to filling up the gas tank of your car. When it's full, you are moving; when it's empty, it's difficult to get going at all. Just take a look at the USDA food pyramid (see page 135) for the suggested number of servings each day. Too many high-fat foods and carbohydrates can slow your down.

I thought that sugary foods gave me a great energy buzz at midafternoon, but I wondered why an hour later I was dragging again. Then I was off to get a soda, and the cycle would repeat itself. One of the best things I learned was to eat smaller meals throughout the day. I always have a healthy snack at midmorning and again in the afternoon. Doing this helps keep my blood sugar level even throughout the day.

At work, I always keep nonperishable foods in my desk drawer—trail mix, rice cakes, pretzels, Fig Newtons, and fruit. When I need a healthy snack, I reach in the drawer instead of making a trip to the candy machine. The more convenient you make healthy eating, the more likely you are to eat healthy.

Oh, and don't think skipping meals is going to help you lose weight. It just places your energy reserves on low. So don't skip meals, especially breakfast.

When is the best time of day to exercise?

Whenever you can! Some people say morning is the best time to work out, some say lunchtime, and others say midafternoon. If you work and/or have kids, the perfect time is whenever you can find time.

Many people are successful working out in the morning. Now that is what I call dedication! In the beginning, I did the morning routine because my work schedule sometimes kept me at the office late. Working out in the morning really wakes you up and gets your metabolism going. You will feel great all day. It all comes down to exercising when you can and when you will stick with it.

What if I stop exercising for a week or two?

How do you get back on track after stopping exercising for a while? First, you need to start back slowly and not jump right in where you left off. It will take a few days to get back into a routine. Try to figure out and record why you got off track—what was going on in your life and with your health. This will help you set up strategies to prevent it from happening again. When you know what the obstacles are, you can determine what you need to do to avoid them.

When I broke my foot six days after finishing my first triathlon, I had a cast on for eight weeks. I thought it was all over—I'd ruined everything, and I was going to lose the fitness I'd worked so hard to achieve.

My coach, Troy Jacobson, explained, "Sure, after about two weeks of no exercise, you will start to lose some of your fitness. It continues to decrease each week you are away from it. The light at the end of the tunnel is that you have already changed your neuromuscular body structure." Huh?

"Well, the muscles have memory," he said. "It will take a while to get back your fitness, but it will come back faster than when you first started."

I remember learning something similar with tap dancing. I would work over and over on one step and not be able to get it, then finally, one day, I could do it. The choreographer said, "Now your muscle remembers."

So take it easy and slow getting back into your routine.

How can I exercise when I have no energy?

You will need to determine whether you are actually tired physically or just bored with your exercise routine. Are you eating properly and getting enough sleep? Check with your doctor if the problem persists, just to rule out other medical issues.

If your doctor gives you the go-ahead, maybe it's time to look for a new incentive—another exercise routine, a new goal, or some friends to exercise with for support.

When you exercise, you are actually giving your body energy. Sometimes it helps to remember how good you feel when you are working out and that afterglow when you are done. Often at the end of a long day, the last thing I want to do is exercise. But I talk to myself about why I am doing this, how good it will feel to get outside, and how accomplished I'll feel when I'm done. On the days when my mind is saying no to exercise, I either take it slow or try something different. That is one of the great reasons to cross-train. It's tough to get bored when there are always new exercises and activities you can try.

How do I start running?

Slowly! Too much too soon can cause injury and burnout. Running is a great cardio exercise that burns lots of calories, but it is an impact sport, particularly on pavement or sidewalks, which are jarring on the bones and joints. This is especially true if you are overweight.

When I began to train for a 5K (see page 116), I started with walking. As I progressed each week, I added a mixture of walking and jogging. By slowly adding more jogging and less walking to my routine, I got to the point where I didn't need to walk at all and could jog comfortably for thirty minutes.

How can I lose some of the weight on my hips, make my thighs smaller, or stop my arms from jiggling?

I hate to say this, but there are no magic potions or pills for these complaints. Sometimes you are just born with your mother's hips. I remember asking the fitness staff at the health club about losing my hips. I said, "I am losing weight everywhere else, but not my hips."

They said, "That is one of the toughest areas to go. It will take time."

Sometimes it all comes down to the way your body is built. If you have wide hips, you're never going to look like a supermodel. I had to accept the fact that I have a large frame and it's okay to have big hips.

When it comes to spot reducing, the answer is a consistent overall cardio routine, healthy eating, and strength training.

I am too busy to exercise. What can I do?

Time management, setting priorities, and being creative with the time you do have can help you find at least fifteen to thirty minutes for exercise every day. One of the things that helped me was to schedule my exercise time as an appointment.

Ideally, you should exercise anywhere from three to five times a week for thirty to sixty minutes each session. However, recent studies have shown that if you don't have a whole thirty minutes available in your day, you can split that time up into three blocks of ten minutes each and still receive the benefits of moving more. My friend Terry has very little time to work out due his demanding work schedule. He uses high-intensity interval workouts for his aerobic exercise in thirty-minute sessions that are up-tempo and burn a lot of calories.

The key is to be creative with the time you have. Let it be quality time where you are focused on the exercise at hand. Put all your energy into it and then be done. Some people are able to get up a little early each morning to get twenty to thirty minutes of exercise in. Lunchtime is a great opportunity to head outside and walk for twenty to thirty minutes. Or set up a treadmill in front of the TV after dinner.

If you have kids, look for a video that shows you how to do at-home exercises using your baby as part of your routine. Or join a health club that has a nursery for your kids while you work out. To make more of family time after dinner, head outside for a walk as a family.

My dad has a very busy work schedule, but he usually goes to the office a little early during the winter so that he can get in his twenty to thirty minutes of walking when he comes home. During the summer, it's easier because it stays light longer and my mom and dad can walk after dinner. Again, I'm talking about being creative in overcoming your time limitations. It takes a little thought, but even with a hectic schedule, you should be able to find thirty minutes. Take a look at your day and figure out where you can shave some time: one less TV show, one less computer game, skimming the headlines instead of reading the whole morning paper. It's not a sacrifice; it's a healthy life change.

Where can I find athletic wear for my full figure?

Finding workout clothes and sports bras in larger sizes is a challenge. In terms of comfort, look for fabrics that are "wicking" (meaning they pull the sweat away from your body). Cotton is one of the worst fabrics you can wear while working out, since it traps the sweat against your body and makes for a miserable feeling.

You'll probably have the best luck finding workout clothes through catalogs or on line. There are a few good sources out there, such as Lane Bryant and JCPenney. Danskin and Champion offer plus-size athletic clothing. Online,

Junonia.com offers a variety of fitness apparel. I have designed a signature collection of full-figure athletic wear in performance fabrics with Iron Girl (www.iron-girl.com).

What can I do to eat healthy when dining out?

Pick restaurants that have healthy choices on the menu. Ask how things are prepared. Ask for grilled meats and grilled or steamed vegetables. Choose tomato sauce over Alfredo, vinaigrette instead of ranch dressing, sorbet instead of ice cream.

For fast food, go for Subway instead of McDonald's. At Wendy's, choose a baked potato and chili instead of a cheeseburger.

Sometimes when I order, I ask questions about how the food is prepared and request low-calorie alternatives (such as having the pasta boiled in water with no added butter or oil). When the food comes, ask for a take-out container right away and place half the meal in it. You will eat less, have better portion control, and not continue to eat if the food is off the plate. The leftovers will make a nice lunch for the next day.

How do I stay motivated?

Motivation has to come from within. You have to have given some thought and planning to your goals. You need to be clear about why you want to get healthy and lose weight.

Some of the things that can help keep you going are having a realistic plan for exercise, finding exercises that are fun, exercising to music, being around people with similar goals, keeping a log to review your progress, reading about others' success stories, and having someone to work out with.

The game to stay motivated is both mental and emotional. Be creative, reward yourself, and remember why you are doing all this. Your health is in your control.

How many calories are in a pound?

Thirty-five hundred. Theoretically, if you take five hundred calories out of your intake each day for a week, you can lose a pound. Exercising for twenty to thirty minutes burns two hundred to three hundred calories.

What other things besides exercise can I do to burn calories?

When you don't have structured exercise time available, remember that you are burning calories all day long. Doing household chores, mowing the lawn, shoveling snow, gardening, walking the dog, taking the stairs instead of the elevator, parking at the far end of the lot—all these burn calories. Add a little zip to everything you do, and you'll burn even a few more calories.

Should I stretch before exercising?

Yes and no. It is recommended that you warm up for five to ten minutes before starting your exercise routine, then do some gentle stretches before continuing. Stretching when your muscles are cold can actually tighten them up or even tear them. When walking or running, it's best to start out slow, then increase your pace as your muscles warm up. Stretch gently after your workout.

How can I control my eating?

Drink two glasses of water a half hour before you eat.

Slow down and stretch the meal out. Try to eat for at least twenty minutes. It takes your brain that long to realize you are satisfied. There are several tricks for doing this.

- After three bites of food, take a sip of water to create a sense of fullness in the stomach and prevent overeating.
- If you use the right hand to eat, switch to the left to slow down the eating process.
- Don't watch TV, read, or work while eating.
- Eat in a separate area or dining room—a place where all you do is eat—then sit and focus on eating. Don't go into that room except at mealtimes.
- Place one serving on your plate. Make sure it's a reasonable portion, and use a smaller plate so the dish looks full. Make it pretty, using garnishes and placing the food attractively on the plate. Don't go back for more.

Hitting the road. Lauri Levenfeld, Zoom Photography, California

• When eating, don't wear sweats or loose-fitting clothes. Stick to normal clothes so you won't overstuff yourself.

• Always leave a little something on the plate. It's a sign of etiquette and not pigging out.

How can I be safe when exercising outside?

Safety is a huge factor when exercising outside. You will need to take some precautions and stay aware of your surroundings.

• When running or walking, go against the oncoming traffic so you can see cars coming toward you.

• Try to run or walk on sidewalks when you can. Stay out of the street.

• Never wear a personal radio or tape player, as you won't be able to hear the traffic around you. Save the music for the treadmill or lap track.

• Wear bright colors so you are visible. In low-light conditions (early morning, dusk, dark days, and at night), wear reflective materials or a reflective vest so you can be seen.

• When out biking, always wear a helmet. Make sure you are riding *with* the traffic, and try to stay to the far side of the road. Remember, as a cyclist you must follow all the rules of the road. Don't try to run stoplights or stop signs. Use hand signals when you are turning.

• Anytime you head outside, let someone know how long you will be gone and where you are planning to go. Don't forget to check back in.

• Vary your route. Stay out of unfamiliar areas and places where you feel uncomfortable.

• Carry identification, a little money, and even a cell phone.

• Go with a buddy.

Final Words

I hope that the stories and ideas in this book have given you a new outlook on how you can have a healthy lifestyle. The process to discover how you can get healthier is just that—a process. You'll have lots of ups and downs along the way. Some days you will stray; you'll eat a doughnut or not exercise. But the next day, you have the chance to begin again.

Making changes to your lifestyle requires patience. Value yourself. Your health is worth the effort.

My pursuit of health came after many years of struggling with my weight and failed diets. In January 1996, when my doctor described me in my chart as "morbidly obese," my weight was no longer about a certain dress size, vanity, or how I looked to others. I knew I had to make some serious changes in my life for the sake of my health.

I have learned that there are no pills, magic fixes, or instant weight-loss programs to manage my weight. I made a decision to do it the old-fashioned way—to eat right and exercise. I've found success by focusing on my health, not my dress size or the scale, and by focusing on making gradual lifestyle changes that will last a lifetime. I started by learning about nutrition, setting goals, finding out the role of food in my life, and adding exercise to my day. Each week, I added a little more.

Part of getting healthy is learning to manage all aspects of your life—the physical, emotional, and spiritual. Become more aware of yourself—your needs, habits, and strengths—and learn to celebrate your victories along the way. Remember that each step you take to make your life healthier is a victory now and for the future.

Now get out the door and start moving. Your mind and body will thank you. Believe that you can do it—because I know you can!

Resources

Nutrition

American Dietetic Association
216 West Jackson Boulevard
Chicago, IL 60606-6995
(312) 899-0040
(800) 366-1655 (nutrition
hotline and referral program)
www.eatright.org
Information on nutrition and
finding a registered dietitian
in your area.

Health

American Medical Women's
Association
801 North Fairfax Street,
Suite 400
Alexandria, VA 22314
(703) 838-0500

Cancer Information Service
(800) 422-6237

American Cancer Society
1599 Clifton Road NE
Atlanta, GA 30329
(800) 227-2345
www.cancer.org

National Osteoporosis
Foundation
1150 17th Street NW,
Suite 500
Washington, DC 20036
(202) 223-2226
www.nfo.org

Arthritis Foundation
1330 West Peachtree Street
Atlanta, GA 30309
(800) 283-7800
www.arthritis.org

Asthma and Allergy
Foundation
(800) 727-8462

American Lung Association
(800) LUNG-USA
www.lungusa.org

American Diabetes
Association
(800) 342-2383
www.diabetes.org

National Headache
Foundation
428 West St. James Place,
2nd Floor
Chicago, IL 60614-2750
(800) 843-2256

American Council for
Headache Education
19 Mantua Road
Mt. Royal, NJ 08061
(800) 255-2243
www.achenet.org

American Heart Association
(800) 242-8721
www.americanheart.org

National Heart, Lung, and
Blood Institute
Information Center
PO Box 30105
Bethesda, MD 20824-1223
(800) 575-WELL

National Women's Health
Resource Center
(877) 986-9472
www.healthywomen.org

Aging

National Institute on Aging
PO Box 8057
Gaithersburg, MD 20898
(800) 222-2225

Eating Disorders

National Association of
    Anorexia Nervosa and
    Associated Disorders
PO Box 7
Highland Park, IL 60035
(847) 831-3438

Overeaters Anonymous
World Service Office
PO Box 44020
Rio Rancho, NM 87174-
    4020
www.overeatersanonymous.
    org

Fitness

American College of Sports
    Medicine
PO Box 1440
Indianapolis, IN 46202
(317) 637-9200

President's Council on
    Physical Fitness and Sports
200 Independence Avenue
    SW, Room 739-H
Washington, DC 20201
(202) 690-9000

Women's Sports Foundation
Eisenhower Park
East Meadow, NY 11554
(800) 227-3988

Heart Rate Monitor Training

Polar Electro, Inc.
370 Crossways Park Drive
Woodbury, NY 11797-2050
www.polarusa.com

Race Events

Active USA
www.activeusa.com
Online information about
finding and registering for
events across the country.

RaceGate
www.racegate.com
Online information about
finding and registering for
events across the country.

Runner's World magazine
www.runnersworld.com
Website and magazine for
issues and topics related to
running; offers race calendar
of running events.

Road Runners Club of
    America (RRCA)
1150 South Washington
    Street
Alexandria, VA 22314
(703) 836-0558
www.rrca.org
Website offers race calendar of
running events and clubs.

Avon Running Global
    Women's Circuit
1345 Avenue of the Americas,
    26th Floor
New York, NY 10105
(212) 282-5350
www.avon.running.com
National race website.

Race for the Cure
(800) 462-9273
www.raceforthecure.com
National race website for the
largest 5K series in the United
States.

Triathlete magazine
www.triathletemag.com
Website and magazine for
issues and topics related to the
sport of triathlon.
Offers race calendar of
triathlon events.

(continued)

Inside Triathlon magazine
www.insidetri.com
Website and magazine for
issues and topics related to the
sport of triathlon.
Offers race calendar of
triathlon events.

Multi-Sport School of
    Champions
www.multisports.com
Multi-Sport School of
Champions represents a
collection of instructional
services aimed at multisport
athletes of all ages,
backgrounds, levels of ability.

Troy Jacobson Multisport
www.coachtroy.com
Camp to assist all levels of
individuals competing in
triathlons.

Team Clydesdale
www.teamclydesdale.com
Organization devoted to
athletes of size competing in
running, triathlon, and
duathlon events.

Challenged Athletes
    Foundation
(619) 793-9393
www.challengedathletes.org
Organization for disabled
athletes who compete in
sports; also offers events.

Swimming

Total Immersion Swim Camp
www.totalimmersion.net
Assists all levels of individuals
in learning or improving their
swimming.

Walking

Prevention Walking Club
PO Box 7488
Red Oak, IA 51591
(800) 666-1216

Walkers Club of America
33 Saddle Lane
Levittown, NY 11756
(516) 579-WALK

North American Racewalk
    Foundation
PO Box 18323
Boulder, CO 80308

March of Dimes Walks
(888) MODIMES
www.modimes.org
Organization that sponsors
10K walking events across the
country to raise money for
research to prevent birth
defects.